Why We Think the Things We Think

Philosophy in a Nutshell

By the same author:

This Book Will Make You Think

The 25 Rules of Grammar

Why We Think the Things We Think

Philosophy in a  Nutshell

ALAIN STEPHEN

Michael O'Mara Books Limited

First published in Great Britain in 2015 by
Michael O'Mara Books Limited
9 Lion Yard
Tremadoc Road
London SW4 7NQ

A CIP catalogue record for this book is available from the British Library.

Papers used by Michael O'Mara Books Limited are natural, recyclable products made from wood grown in sustainable forests. The manufacturing processes conform to the environmental regulations of the country of origin.

ISBN: 978-1-78243-413-9 in hardback print format
ISBN: 978-1-78243-411-5 in ebook format

2 3 4 5 6 7 8 9 10

Designed and typeset by K. DESIGN, Winscombe, Somerset

Printed and bound in Great Britain by CPI Group (UK) Ltd, Croydon, CR0 4YY

www.mombooks.com

For Polly

Contents

Introduction: philosophy in a nutshell?

One of my earliest memories is of sitting in my bedroom in my parents' house bereft of anything in particular to do. The antique train-set, beautifully landscaped and papier-mâchéd in puce green (it had a tunnel through a mountain and two stations), which was bolted to the wall and took up almost half the room, had broken down. In truth, it was always breaking down, but it was a joy when it worked. I think it was then that I started thinking about how things work, or don't work, at some times but not others. I was not pondering this in the mundane sense, such as of a washing machine breaking down, or of dropping a mobile phone in a toilet, nor even of my train set that had worked perfectly the day before. Instead, I was developing a sense of the fallible nature of things in general.

What is at the core of this transient nature of reality that my six-year-old self was struggling to comprehend? I would hardly call it a eureka moment, but I suddenly realized that I was having a conversation with myself. I was asking questions, analysing, deliberating and, quite frankly, feeling confused. As far back as my memory serves, that seems to be the point when I first started thinking, or was conscious of being able to think, for myself.

Of course, I must have been thinking before that. I must *have known* not to put my hand in the open fire, or to stand in front of a bus, or to leave my bicycle out in the rain. I must *have known* what it was like to feel hungry or happy or angry or sad. Was this knowledge *a priori* (a term many philosophers are particularly keen on), meaning had I acquired this knowledge from my innate capacity for theoretical deduction, as opposed to observation of my own experiences? This 'voice in my head' was starting to ask questions – why is there a voice in our heads? I've used the word 'known' several times in this paragraph, in the present perfect tense most commonly used to denote unfinished time. But what would happen if time suddenly stopped; if it finished? Would every voice in everyone's head suddenly stop thinking? It is a pretty fearful thought.

How long I sat thinking under the broken train set in my bedroom I don't know. One thing that has always struck me is how our personal perception of time and space seems to narrow and reduce as we get older. An hour, a day, even a month seems much longer to a six-year-old than to a forty-six-year-old. The summer holidays seem to last an age when you are an adolescent, but these days all I notice is how early the street lights go on in August. I remember returning to my old secondary school a couple of years after I had left and being struck by how small the school hall suddenly seemed. This space, with its imposing wooden stage at one end where the austere headmaster delivered his assemblies, flanked by rows of senior teachers, appeared vast when I was in the first form. It suddenly seemed to have got smaller, its dimensions had shrunk. Unless the school had undertaken radical building work, this wasn't possible. It was simply that my perception of the space or, more pertinently, my experience of myself within that space had changed.

So what relevance does a broken train set or a shrinking school hall have for the subject of philosophy? Both these phenomena represent observations and reflections from experience. How reliable these reflections are when filtered through the prism of memories is open to question. I am attempting, in a roundabout way, to come to some conclusions about what actually constitutes philosophy. Is it thinking and reflecting on the human experience of reality?

The traditional definition of a philosopher (often attributed to Pythagoras) is a 'lover of wisdom or knowledge'. It would follow that philosophy is the study of knowledge. It is interesting to note how philosophy and science as disciplines devoted to understanding the world have separated and diverged over the last few centuries. Science seems to hold the upper hand, since it seems able to prove things. Philosophy is seen in some senses as purely theoretical, adept at asking questions but incapable of providing clear answers. Many of the great philosophers did not distinguish between the importance of disciplines such as mathematics, physics and the natural sciences over the study of ethics, aesthetics or theology. Immanuel Kant once famously asserted that philosophy was 'the queen of all the sciences' – he thought that studying thoughts and ideas or, more precisely, how ideas are formed, was of higher importance than doing sums or solving equations. The common cliché is that philosophy is comprised of questions of which the answer is invariably more questions. In this light, is it possible to present philosophy 'in a nutshell'?

This book has its work cut out, as it is composed of questions. These questions, it is hoped, will have occurred to most people from time to time, especially during quiet moments of reflection or observation (like my younger self sat under the train set).

I have been necessarily selective in the philosophers I have chosen to elucidate the questions, and have tried, where possible, to provide counter-arguments and perspectives. Fundamental questions such as 'what is happiness?' have been examined by many philosophers and writers through the ages, and to attempt a comprehensive review of all of the literature on the subject would, of course, fill a library. I apologize for any omissions, and hope my summaries will encourage you to further investigate the questions. Many of the key ideas and issues overlap, so I have attempted to signpost where relationships exist. There are undoubtedly many related ideas in the study of ethics, aesthetics and systems of belief. We owe it to ourselves never to stop trying to learn new things or, more importantly, to question why some things are, and other things are not. Maybe the right to examine ideas and thoughts is philosophy in a nutshell.

Alain Stephen

Why is there something rather than nothing?

Metaphysics is a branch of philosophy that addresses questions concerning the nature of existence and relationships between mind and matter. The word first appears in the works of the Ancient Greek philosopher Aristotle (384–322 BCE) as *metaphusika,* meaning 'after physics'. This has led to the common interpretation of metaphysics as the study of things beyond the physical world, or of things that cannot be analysed through scientific experiment, observation or method. There is a theory that Aristotle's use of the word can be attributed to the first editor of his collected works, Andronicus of Rhodes. Aristotle wrote treatises on a vast range of subjects and the word *metaphusika* was Andronicus' method of classifying a series of writings that were not concerned with disciplines such as science, mathematics or law.

However, subsequent philosophers have taken the term to mean the study of the non-physical or immaterial, and relationships with perceived reality. Aristotle was particularly fond of ordering different branches of human knowledge. According to Andronicus, he valued metaphysics as the purest of the sciences, using the term 'first principles' to denote the discovery of the essential laws that govern the universe.

> ❝ Nothing is more real than nothing. ❞
>
> SAMUEL BECKETT, *MALONE DIES* (1956)

One of the central issues of metaphysics concerns defining the 'nature' of being, existence and our sense of reality. One aspect of these enquiries concerns the question of why there is something rather than nothing. The pre-Socratic Ancient Greek philosopher Parmenides of Elea (*c.* 515–460 BCE) addressed the issue in his treatise, *On Nature*. Parmenides' investigation takes the form of an epic poem, of which only one hundred and sixty lines remain (it is thought the original work contained over three thousand lines). The poem outlines the story of a young man (presumably Parmenides) meeting a goddess who imparts to him the true nature of all things in the universe. The goddess explains that there are two fundamental ways of understanding: the way of truth and the way of opinion.

The way of truth is defined as things as they are and this can be delineated into two paths of enquiry: things that exist and things that don't exist. For Parmenides, we know that things exist because it is impossible to contemplate something that doesn't exist, just as it is impossible for nothing to become something:

> *It is necessary to speak and to think what is; for being is, but nothing is not.*
>
> PARMENIDES, *ON NATURE* (*c.* 475 BCE)

In contrast to the way of truth is the way of opinion. Parmenides takes issue with earlier pre-Socratic thinkers' reliance upon the senses to determine the nature of things, by arguing that the senses are unreliable. In short, our experience of things is different from things 'as they are' (see *Can we ever experience anything objectively?*) and so cannot be trusted. Thus, Parmenides can be considered one of the first thinkers to express the duality between appearances and reality.

Parmenides concludes that as what is *is*, and what is not cannot be, there is something rather than nothing, because nothing doesn't exist. The universe is therefore one single, infinite, eternal and unchanging entity. The English philosopher Bertrand Russell provides a neat summary of Parmenides' paradox in his famous work, *A History of Western Philosophy*:

> *When you think, you think of something;*
> *when you use a name, it must be the name*
> *of something. Therefore both thought and*
> *language require objects outside themselves.*
> *And since you can think of a thing or speak*
> *of it at one time as well as another, whatever*
> *can be thought of or spoken of must exist*
> *at all times. Consequently there can be no*
> *change, since change consists in things*
> *coming into being or ceasing to be.*
>
> BERTRAND RUSSELL, *A HISTORY OF WESTERN*
> *PHILOSOPHY* (1945)

In his influential lecture 'What Is Metaphysics?', the German existential philosopher Martin Heidegger attempted to reverse the focus of Parmenides' paradox. For Heidegger, metaphysics had concentrated too much on an analysis of 'what is', whilst neglecting to ask the question 'what is not?'.

Heidegger points out that in order to fully contemplate the nature of 'nothing' we need to set aside formal logic and Parmenides' assertion that it is impossible to comprehend that which doesn't exist. Heidegger takes an abstract, quasi-psychological approach to the problem of nothing.

> *Carefully contemplating Nothing in itself, we begin to notice the importance and vitality of our own moods. Above all else, Nothing is what produces in us a feeling of dread.*
>
> MARTIN HEIDEGGER, 'WHAT IS METAPHYSICS?'
> (LECTURE AT THE UNIVERSITY OF FREIBURG,
> GERMANY, 24 JULY 1929)

This deep feeling of dread, Heidegger held, is the most fundamental human clue to the nature and reality of nothing. Heidegger uses the term *Dasein*, which roughly translates as 'being there' or existing, to describe human life, but asserts that our *Dasein* is temporal and uncertain. The fact that at some point we will die and cease to be is therefore a feature of our human experiences. Heidegger argues that if death, in some counter-intuitive way defines life, so too nothing provides form to something. In this respect, being is not the opposite of nothing: the two states are parallel and related. This led Heidegger to suggest that the principle subject of philosophical discussion is not 'why is there something rather than nothing?' but rather 'why is there something and nothing in the first place?'

What is morality?

Traditionally, there are two uses of the word 'morality'. A descriptive definition relates to specific codes of conduct put forth by a society, organization or social group as an accepted model of individual behaviour. A normative definition relates to codes of conduct that, in line with certain conditions, would be adhered to by all rational beings. How the term morality is applied is essential in the formulation of a key branch of philosophy known as ethics. Normative morality seeks to unearth a universal code of conduct that applies to all persons who can understand it and can govern their behaviour by it. This code should be binding, and require that persons refrain from acting in a manner that violates a moral proscription. An example of this would be the ethical prohibition that it is wrong to end another person's life. Furthermore, normative morality requires adherence to a set of valid conditions by which rational persons are able to sanction the code. For example, although it is wrong to end another person's life, are there certain conditions that would nonetheless make it morally the right thing to do?

Moral theories vary in their analysis of the key aspects of rational persons and in their qualifications of the circumstances in which all rational persons would approve a code of conduct as a moral code (see *How can we tell the difference between right and wrong?*). One of the major issues in moral philosophy concerns the debate between moral realism and anti-realism.

Moral realist philosophers take the view that there are objective moral facts. In other words, that there are things in the world which are always good or bad, independent of an individual's point of view. The counterargument – the anti-realist position – is that there are no absolute moral facts, merely opinions, and what we consider to be moral facts are not rules we discover but rules we invent for ourselves. Related to this debate is an issue about what is termed cognitivism and non-cognitivism, and the validity of moral statements. Cognitivism states that declarations about moral issues are propositions and as such can be tested by reason to determine whether they are true or false. For example, take the statement 'murder is wrong'. In making the declaration about murder I have described something about the world. Furthermore, I have applied the value of 'wrongness' to the concept of murder. In order to determine if murder indeed has the value of wrongness, I need to come to a conclusion about its objective validity – is the description right or wrong?

❛ Never let your sense of morals get
in the way of doing what's right. ❜

ISAAC ASIMOV, *FOUNDATION* (1951)

Non-cognitivism takes the opposite position. According to non-cognitivists, when I make the statement 'murder is wrong', I am not describing the world in objective terms but merely expressing my own feelings and opinions. Non-cognitivism therefore claims that because moral statements are not descriptive they can be neither true nor false. Logically, for something to be true it needs to be described as being the way that it is, or conversely, to be false it needs to be described as being other than the way that it is. Non-descriptive statements can't be either true or false.

Non-cognitivism has led to a further development in meta-ethics, known as expressivism. According to expressivism, the meaning of moral language is not to describe things or state clearly defined facts about the world but rather *to express* an evaluation in the form of an attitude or observation. Thus, statements such as 'torturing kittens is bad' contain no statement of fact and therefore have no truth-value. This led to a major puzzle in semantics when a simple moral declarative sentence is embedded into a more complex sentence. Consider the following argument:

> *Torturing kittens is bad.*
> *If torturing kittens is bad then it is wrong to ask your friends to torture kittens.*
> *Therefore it is wrong to ask your friends to torture kittens.*

The first sentence, according to expressivism, has no truth-value and is just an evaluation of the act of torturing kittens. In the second sentence, however, a hypothetical scenario is set up which does not express an evaluation of torturing kittens; it merely satisfies a condition. According to formal propositional logic (known as *modus ponens*), if the first part of a statement or proposition implies a second part and the first proposition is taken to be true, the second part must also be true. Thus, the expressivism theory cannot be applied to the second sentence but formal logic can, regardless of an absence of truth-values. This problem is known as the Frege-Geach objection, after the twentieth-century British philosopher Peter Geach's analysis of the works of the German philosopher and mathematician Gottlob Frege (1848–1925).

One possible way around the problem of the truth-value of moral statements is to look at the intention behind moral judgements and how they are expressed in language. What is the speaker intending to achieve by the statement 'torturing kittens is bad' and how does this reflect the speaker's mental (cognitive) state? Just as statements express our ordinary ideas and beliefs about the world, they also express moral judgements and beliefs. In this sense morality becomes as much a matter of the usage of moral language as a traditional code of conduct, an area that modern philosophy increasingly tries to address. Ultimately, although the possibility of being deceived by moral judgements is bad from an individual perspective, it would be worse if we were to deceive ourselves into accepting moral facts as truths simply because of the way in which they are expressed.

❝ Men, I think, are not capable of doing nothing, of saying nothing, of not reacting to injustice, of not protesting against oppression, of not striving for the good society and the good life in the ways they see it. ❞

NELSON MANDELA (1918–2013)

Do we have free will?

A broad definition of philosophy is that it is concerned with discovering the fundamental nature of knowledge, reality and existence. If we take 'knowledge' as being compatible with 'meaning' and 'understanding' then this definition can be simplified as the quest to understand the meaning of life. One area that has consistently troubled philosophers engaged in the search for meaning is the extent to which we are in control of our lives. Fundamental to this question is the problem of free will.

A neutral definition of free will is *the distinctive capacity of agents (persons) to make choices over the course of their actions. Related to these choices are notions of right and wrong and issues related to ethics, moral responsibility and accountability of conduct.* The problem of free will is that it stands in direct contradiction to the doctrine of *determinism.*

Determinism is a far-reaching concept with radical implications for science, religion, ethics and the law. The common explanation of determinism is that every action or event in the world is caused by or is the result of antecedent factors. This perspective posits the notion that reality is already pre-determined or pre-existent and, therefore, nothing new can ever occur as all events are simply the effects of other prior effects. If determinism is correct, then just as all events in the present are inevitable and unalterable, so too will be all events in the future. Under such conditions, the exercise of free will or freedom of choice in the strictest sense is at best an illusion, because all of our actions are 'products' of factors beyond our control. Or in other words, all events must have a cause, which determines the outcome.

A form of determinism originated with the philosophers of the 'atomist school' of Ancient Greece, such as Democritus and Epicurus (see *Is too much better than not enough?*), although the 'atomists' were less concerned with examining the problem of free will than with dispelling prevailing superstitions about destiny and fate. Modern determinism has its roots in developments in science in the eighteenth and nineteenth centuries. Within determinism are several sub-divisions, such as physical determinism, which reduces human relationships to the interaction of biological, chemical or physical properties and has been key to the growth of neuropsychology. Historical determinism (or historical materialism) forms the basis of the political philosophy of Karl Marx, and relates to functions of economics.

The common approach to analysing the problem of free will versus determinism has taken the form of an in-depth examination of definitions and complexities inherent in the use of terms such as 'free', 'will', 'cause' and 'choice'. By struggling to define exactly what free will entails, philosophers have grappled with ideas such as 'the capacity to do otherwise' or 'optional possibilities'. This foregrounding, and the meanings signified by the language deployed, has led to the suspicion amongst some modern philosophers that the problem is purely a matter of semantics and therefore a pseudo-problem. In response, other thinkers have analysed the complexity of decision-making, and the significance of linguistic nuances when discussing free will.

One argument against determinism is provided by a perspective known as *metaphysical libertarianism*, which posits that free will does exist in certain individuals. In his essay 'The Will to Believe', the nineteenth-century American philosopher and psychologist William James (1842–1910) argued that free will existed simply because he had chosen to believe it to be so. This observation led on to a detailed analysis of the nature of choice, and in particular the human capacity to consciously deny or affirm a course of action or conflicting desire.

❛ If God did not exist, it would be necessary to invent him. ❜

VOLTAIRE, EPISTLE TO THE AUTHOR OF THE BOOK, *THE THREE IMPOSTORS* (1768)

In *Leviathan* (1651), the English philosopher Thomas Hobbes held that liberty (he avoided the use of the term free will) was simply the absence of external impediments to action. For Hobbes, free will exists as long as we are not externally constrained or coerced. This view is echoed by contemporary philosophers such as the American Richard Rorty, who make clear the difference between freedom of 'will' and freedom of action, thereby distinguishing between freedom of having 'optional possibilities' from the freedom to endorse those choices.

It could be argued that all humans intuit (rightly or wrongly) a sense of free will or of 'the self'. Modern psychology acknowledges, to some degree, the conflict of free will with the formation of our character and modes of behaviour. Determinism certainly presents a bleak proposition. Think about it. All of our actions and thoughts are causally determined. Is there an alternative? Can actions or thoughts be un-caused? Modern science, from Darwin to quantum mechanics, have focused on randomness and the notion that the extent of our influence is in the probability or indeterminacy of things. This has not, however, fully dismantled the dilemmas of determinism, for randomness can only ever suggest the possibility of free will and is no more a proof than a belief in the pre-determined nature of all things.

Bernard Bolzano (1781–1848) and Franz Exner (1802–1880) were both professors of philosophy and theology at Prague University in the 1830s who conducted a long-running debate on the question of free will and determinism. Bolzano, a Catholic priest, was something of a radical who held strong views on a variety of subjects, most pertinently on the immorality and futility of war and conflict. Bolzano and Exner decided that the truth of determinism couldn't be based on statistics and mathematics, as these concerned the mere probability of facts, rather than facts themselves. Bolzano was eventually dismissed from his teaching post because the Austrian authorities that paid his salary considered his radical ideas too subversive. In the late 1840s, however, Austria underwent a period of reform which aimed to weaken the hegemony of the Catholic Church, especially in state institutions. Franz Exner was then able to help to change the educational curriculum in universities, and one of his first proposals was for probability to be taught as a means for students to understand and take responsibility and control of their lives: to exercise free will.

Is beauty in the eye of the beholder?

Aesthetics is the field of philosophical investigation that addresses the nature of beauty. What is it that makes something beautiful? What mysterious combination of elements and forms combine to define something as being beautiful, as opposed to anodyne, ugly or dull? The arbitrary argument is that beauty is entirely subjective, a matter wholly of personal taste. At least in philosophical terms, this line of reasoning is a false conclusion, as it gives no clear definition of the factors that determine personal taste and, moreover, how we acquired our aesthetic sensibilities in the first place.

Aesthetics, as with virtually all branches of Western philosophy, has its roots in Ancient Greece, most notably in the work of Plato (c. 428–348 BCE). The question 'what is beauty?' was addressed by Plato in his work *Hippias Major*, which forms part of his collection of famous *dialogues*. Plato recounts a discussion between his teacher Socrates and the sophist Hippias. Socrates tells Hippias (a rather vain and arrogant man) that he had recently been exposed in an argument by an unnamed antagonist for not offering a clear definition of the nature of beauty, and invites Hippias to proffer an opinion. Hippias is flattered by the great Socrates asking for his help and offers three examples of beauty: a beautiful woman, any object made from or adorned with gold, and a long prosperous and healthy life. Socrates dismisses each of Hippias' examples as being merely material examples of superficial beauty for which there are obvious contradictions, and asks the question again: what is beauty in itself? This leads the two men to examine more conceptual notions of beauty such as 'is beauty that which is convenient, useful or beneficial according to different circumstances?' Again, Socrates exposes the flaws in each example and finally decides that beauty could be related to the senses – the sights, sounds and smells that provoke pleasure – albeit remaining sceptical whether this is actually a precise definition of beauty.

Although the dialogue recounted in *Hippias Major* doesn't arrive at a clear conclusion about the nature of beauty, it suggests that beauty could be something in and of itself. This led Plato to view beauty as one of his ideal forms – a representation of divine perfection. Greek art during this golden age centred on representations of the human form as gods or mythical heroes, icons to be worshipped, loved and revered. Socrates' suggestion that beauty is that which excites pleasure in the senses concurs with the Ancient Greek view of love as the highest state of human consciousness.

The correlation between love and beauty is further explored in Plato's *Symposium* – the most ambitious of his dialogues in that it takes place at a party and contains multiple participants analysing philosophical propositions. The section of the *Symposium* dedicated to beauty is contained in the speech of Diotima.

In the *Symposium*, Socrates relates a speech by the priestess Diotima, whom he introduces as an expert in love. Diotima describes how a true appreciation of erotics entails moving from the love of an attractive, beautiful body and individual to an appreciation of beauty itself. This step-by-step transformation is known as Plato's *scala amoris* or 'ladder of love'. The highest form of love cannot be reached without having previously ascended the lower rungs of the ladder; that is, having experienced physical attraction. A popular interpretation of climbing this metaphorical ladder is that the lover abandons all the previous objects of their affection and ardour as they journey towards an ultimate understanding of beauty in itself.

Both Plato and Socrates seem to be siding with a subjectivist approach with regards to beauty: that all knowledge, and therefore by extension our knowledge of beauty, is defined by the experiences of the self and our sensory perceptions. In this respect, beauty is in the eye of the beholder. As stated previously, though (and in an aspect of the question 'what is beauty?' that clearly troubled Socrates), this still doesn't get very far with determining exactly what combination of factors define something as 'beautiful'.

❛ The best part of beauty is that
which no picture can express. ❜

SIR FRANCIS BACON, 'OF BEAUTY' (1612)

David Hume (1711–1776), the Scottish philosopher
and historian, attempted to analyse this problem in
his essay 'Of the Standard of Taste' (1757). Hume
was concerned with critical judgements and how one
critical pronouncement can hold sway over another,
contrary point of view. One of the major issues clouding
critical judgement, according to Hume, is an inability
to distinguish between matters of fact and expressions
of sentiment. For example, an ardent supporter of a
particular football team may witness a goal scored by
their team that exhibits skill, balance and athleticism
and pronounce it 'beautiful'. If the opposition scores a
goal of comparable merit it is unlikely to provoke the
same response. This is because their initial judgement
is coloured by sentiment and therefore prejudiced.
Verdicts based on sentiment are devoid of any
discernible truth-value and thus rendered, in Hume's
words, 'absurd and ridiculous'.

For Hume, matters of taste and critical judgements are
often determined by slight differences and oppositions
and yet, in general, people recognize and respond to
more obvious aspects and qualities. How many times

have people expressed pleasure at the sight of a sunset, yet the sun sets every day so why should one be more beautiful than another? To illustrate his point about fine margins of taste, Hume quotes a story from Cervantes' *Don Quixote* (1605). In the story, Sancho Panza describes two men tasting a barrel of wine that they have been told is amongst the finest in all of Spain. The first man samples the wine with the tip of his tongue and concurs that it is of good quality but has a hint of iron. The second man smells the wine, agrees that it is of high vintage but that it has a hint of leather in its bouquet. Some onlookers ridicule the two men and dismiss their judgements, accusing them of making false criticisms. When all the wine is finished, however, a rusty key and a leather thong are found in the bottom of the barrel. Hume uses Cervantes' story to illustrate his point that taste is a matter of refinement, needing to be practised in as dispassionate a way as possible. For Hume, aesthetic judgements are not a matter of determining whether one position is true and an alternative position false, but in deciding which position is better than the other. This assessment is possible through applying the following criteria:

> *There is a road from the eye to the heart that does not go through the intellect.*
>
> G.K. CHESTERTON, *THE DEFENDANT* (1901), 'A DEFENCE OF HERALDRY'.

Strong sense, united to delicate sentiment, improved by practice, perfected by comparison, and cleared of all prejudice, can alone entitle critics to this valuable character ...

DAVID HUME, 'OF THE STANDARD OF TASTE' (1757)

In summary, aesthetics has proved to be a fruitful, if beguiling, area of philosophical enquiry throughout the ages. It has tended to throw up more questions than answers and, try as they may, none of the great thinkers have ever quite managed to wriggle away from the subjective position that beauty, and its appreciation, is largely a matter of personal perception.

Can we ever experience anything objectively?

In philosophy there is a clear distinction between the terms 'objectivity' and 'subjectivity'. The object relates to something that exists in time and space, and the subject the being (usually human) with the capacity to perceive the object in its physical form. The issue for philosophers has centred on determining the extent to which the human mind perceives things as they are (objectively), or perceives things how it thinks they are (subjectively). Objectivity in this sense is characteristically related to ideas concerning truth and reality and epistemological problems on the discrepancies between 'objective knowledge' and 'subjective knowledge'.

John Locke (1632–1704) illustrated the difference between subjective perception and objective reality in his famous water bucket experiment. Locke took two buckets of water, one ice cold and the other scalding hot. He then, for a few moments, placed his right hand in the cold bucket and his left hand in the hot bucket. Locke then plunged both hands into a bucket of lukewarm, tepid water. The cold hand provoked the sensation of the tepid bucket being warm whereas the hot hand, conversely, felt cold. Locke surmised that if a single perceiving mind could experience the same 'objective' reality in two different ways, then it followed that two independent perceiving minds can also perceive reality in different ways.

Consider the following scenario: two friends meet up to go for a walk together; one is wearing a heavy winter coat, the other a light summer jacket. They call at the house of a third friend. The third person asks his two friends what the weather is like outside. One friend says it is mild, the other says there is a chill in the air. This presents the third friend with a dilemma as he is presented with two different subjective judgements. The third friend then checks the thermometer on the windowsill, notes a reading of twenty degrees Celsius, and decides that it is warm and pleasant outside so he won't need a heavy coat.

The third friend's judgement was based upon a measurement to provide an objective judgement: twenty degrees is pretty warm for most people. The question here is the extent to which agreement between perceiving subjects constitutes an objective truth: does the fact that two, three, four or more people perceive something as so actually mean that it is? Locke approached this dilemma by drawing a distinction between the *primary* and *secondary* qualities of things.

❝ It is impossible to find an answer which someday will not be found to be wrong. ❞

RICHARD FEYNMAN, 'THE RELATION OF SCIENCE AND RELIGION' (FROM A TALK AT THE CALTECH YMCA LUNCH FORUM, 2 MAY 1956)

Locke was an empiricist thinker who rejected the idea of human beings having been born with innate knowledge. For Locke, the human mind begins with a blank slate or *tabula rasa* that is filled with ideas through experiences. Knowledge is gained through two methods, which Locke termed 'sensation' and 'reflection'. Sensation relates to the five human senses and gives rise to concepts such as sounds, smells, colours, shapes and tastes. Reflection relates to processes in our internal world, thoughts and memories, reasoning and argument. The exercise of our faculties for sensation and reflection gives rise to the formation of simple ideas. These small morsels of knowledge can then be expanded, by combining, comparing or abstracting them into more complex ideas about the world. In short, all ideas, either simple or complex, are born from our experiences. Linked to the formation of ideas is Locke's notion of qualities, which are derived through sensations. A quality, according to Locke, is the aspect of an external object that creates ideas, as we perceive it through our senses. Hence, ideas exist within our minds, whereas qualities exist within objects. Locke divided qualities into two categories. The first category, *primary qualities*, are the aspects that all objects possess, such as size, shape, matter and motion. *Secondary qualities* are aspects which Locke suggests can be either added to or removed from an object, such as colours, sounds, temperatures and textures. The fundamental distinction between the two categories is that primary qualities are inseparable from the object itself, whereas secondary qualities are not. For example, you can cut a plank of wood in half, but it will still retain its primary qualities. However, if you pour a pot of creosote over it, you will change its colour. Locke suggests that because secondary qualities can be added or removed they are relative only to the subject that perceives them.

There are interesting implications in Locke's distinction between primary and secondary qualities, particularly with reference to the human senses. Our sense of the colour of things is produced by tiny particles of light entering the eyes and stimulating the nerves. However, it is not the colour itself that reaches the eyes but particles or photons that have primary qualities of size, shape and motion, even when static. This means that secondary qualities are in essence only the ideas produced by senses when they come into contact with the (primary) particles of objects. For example, by grinding coriander seeds with a pestle and mortar, flavours, colours and aromas will be released. Although visually the seeds have been altered and are now a fine powder rather than solid seeds, the primary qualities of the coriander seeds remain essentially the same, in that it is matter composed of particles.

Therefore the ideas we form from the secondary qualities of things do not resemble the things in the objects themselves. Primary qualities exist in objects, but as our perception of them is limited to the workings of our senses, all we have to go on are impressions of what we think we see, smell, hear, touch and taste, which bears no direct correlation with the qualities of the objects themselves. To ever experience anything objectively we would have to be able to compare things as they really are with our ideas of them, and this is impossible.

What is art?

It is a well-worn cliché to hear people, self-conscious of the knowledge underpinning their opinions, say: 'I don't know much about art, but I know what I like.' Although, for argument's sake, this is a subjective dead end, to some extent it echoes the Platonic view of beauty (see *Is beauty in the eye of the beholder?*). Socrates, according to Plato, defined beauty as that which excites pleasure in the senses. Classical Greek art concerned itself with portrayals of gods and mythical heroes as objects and icons of perfection, thereby endorsing this correlation of art as beauty and beauty as art. This idealized view of art is difficult to apply to, for example, the vivid depictions of violence in religious art of the Renaissance period. Paintings such as Rubens' *Elevation of the Cross*, Grünewald's *The Mocking of Christ* and Caravaggio's *Entombment* portray the torture and execution of Jesus with such lurid intensity that it is difficult to see how anyone could take any sensual pleasure from viewing them. Painted as altarpieces, they were intended to terrify and inform the awful suffering of Christ the martyr. Yet all three painters are acknowledged as great masters of fine art.

In 1897, the Russian novelist Leo Tolstoy wrote a lengthy treatise analysing the question of what exactly constitutes art. *What Is Art?* was initially published in English because it fell foul of the Russian censors, largely on the grounds of Tolstoy expressing several highly contentious opinions. Tolstoy starts by attacking the classical view of art as beauty by arguing that all judgements of beauty are subjective. To take the view that art is beauty as an objective viewpoint requires the assumption that everyone views things the same way. If beauty can be found in the perfection of the natural world, what need is there for art? Tolstoy's main issue is that this view of art is both objective and subjective and fails to answer the core question of what is art.

Tolstoy draws heavily upon the work of French art theorist Eugène Véron and, in particular, Véron's book *L'Esthetique* (1879) for his definition of art. Véron's argument is that although much art can be considered beautiful and pleasing to the senses, beauty is not the principle characteristic of art. Art is more than just pretty pictures or pleasing arrangements of sounds and words. Art is the expression of human ideas and emotions and, moreover, the medium through which these expressions are communicated between people. For Tolstoy, however, it was not enough for art to be just an expression: the expression had to be successful in that the audience, the person(s) viewing the painting or listening to a symphony, must feel the same as the artist who created the work. This standpoint then provides Tolstoy with ample opportunity to list, in iconoclastic fashion, all the 'artists' he doesn't like (Goethe, Beethoven and Shakespeare among them). Tolstoy therefore draws a distinction between 'good art' as that which successfully transmits powerful emotions and ideas and 'bad art', which doesn't, because it is muddled, bogus and confused. Moving a definition of art away from the narrow analysis of beauty as a prerequisite is valid. However, it is hard not to feel that Tolstoy is simply saying 'I know a lot about art and I know what I like', for what one person finds emotionally engaging and a powerful expression could leave another person feeling cold or confused.

Friedrich Nietzsche (1844–1900) attempted to develop a definition of art in his analysis of classical Greek theatre, *The Birth of Tragedy* (1872). Nietzsche proposes that human life is involved in an inexorable struggle between two opposing states of being. Nietzsche names these two opposing forces after the Greek gods Apollo and Dionysus. The *Apollonian* drive is characterized by the visionary power of dreams that manifest in serene forms, such as classical sculptures, the balance of harmonies in musical composition or, to give a modern example, the abstract cubism of Picasso and Mondrian. In contrast, the *Dionysian* drive is one of disorder, intoxication (Dionysus being the Greek god of wine) and frenzy. Dionysian art invokes wild abandon, which Nietzsche exemplifies by the untamed folk dances of medieval festivals. The unchained live performances of the rock guitarist Jimi Hendrix or the nihilistic creations of artist Damien Hirst could be classified as presenting Dionysian elements. However, for Nietzsche, true art derives from the clash between the two opposing forces and occupies the space caused by the tension between them. To return to the examples above, Jimi Hendrix was a highly competent musician with an impeccable grasp of standard blues scales (Apollonian forces), which he subverted by unusual key changes and through the sheer exuberance of his playing style (Dionysian forces). Likewise, Picasso spent years studying the technical aspects of artistic composition before embarking upon his abstract subversions of form and perspective. Nietzsche argues that the serenity and beauty of classical art may appear to be Apollonian in that it promotes order and peace but this should be seen as a reaction to an understanding of darker, oppressive forces that also exist in the world. In his words, 'How much must this people [the Greeks] have suffered to have created such beauty!'

> ❪ Art is either a plagiarist or a revolutionary. ❫
>
> PAUL GAUGUIN (1848–1903), FROM HUNEKER,
> *THE PATHOS OF DISTANCE* (1913)

So, what is art? The Socratic view is that beauty and art are linked because they excite and provoke the senses. Tolstoy rejected this view as being too subjective and looked to art to express human ideas and emotions. Nietzsche examined the Apollonian and Dionysian forces behind these expressions as a way of examining and evaluating artistic endeavours. Rubens' depiction of the crucifixion has elements of both, in that it is by turns magnificent and horrifying. Perhaps Nietzsche comes closest to explaining the mixture of violence and beauty in the religious art of the Renaissance.

> ❛ Things are not all so comprehensible and expressible as one would mostly have us believe; most events are inexpressible, taking place in a realm which no word has ever entered, and more inexpressible than all else are works of art, mysterious existences, the life of which, while ours passes away, endures. ❜
>
> RAINER MARIA RILKE, *LETTERS TO A YOUNG POET* (1929)

Duchamp's Fountain

One of the most famous examples of avant-garde art is Marcel Duchamp's work *Fountain* (1917). The 'sculpture' consisted of a porcelain urinal bought from a plumbing supplies store, which Duchamp submitted for The Society of Independent Artists exhibition in New York. Duchamp is thought to have presented the work as a practical joke and a comment on the pomposity of the art world at the time. Yet *Fountain* has come to be considered by art critics as one of the most influential pieces of the twentieth century, which is curious considering the origins of its conception.

Although many people are familiar with the idea of *Fountain*, hardly anybody has actually seen it. The Society refused to display the urinal at the original exhibition so it was photographed, and then presumably thrown away. In the early 1920s Duchamp's *Fountain* caused much debate about what constitutes art but it is the photograph that people have seen, rather than the 'sculpture' itself. It could be argued that this is a perfect example of art being no more than an idea, however obtuse, and not necessarily an object at all.

How do we know that our experience of consciousness is the same as other people's?

It is a commonly held belief that all human beings are essentially the same on the outside. We all live and breathe, eat and sleep and share identical and necessary biological functions. Many philosophers have argued that the human capacity for conscious thought is the key aspect of our existence that separates us from other animals (see *Do animals have rights?*). We all have an inner life of the mind – thoughts, beliefs, feelings and emotions – and, although we cannot be completely confident that we know what other people are thinking at any given time, we are certain that they have a capacity to experience consciousness very much as we do. But what underpins this certainty? How do we know that others experience the world as we do? Furthermore, how do we know that other minds exist at all? In philosophy, this question is known as 'the problem of other minds' and is linked to the idea of *solipsism*.

> 6 My imagination makes me human and makes me a fool; it gives me all the world and exiles me from it. 9
>
> URSULA LE GUIN, *HARPER'S* MAGAZINE (1990)

Solipsism is the belief that the only thing that truly exists, or more precisely, the only thing that we can *know* exists, is our own minds. The British utilitarian philosopher John Stuart Mill approached the epistemological question of knowing other minds exist in his 1865 essay 'An Examination of Sir William Hamilton's Philosophy'. Mill argued that it was possible to determine the existence of minds other than our own via a process of inference and analogy. Taking as a starting point Descartes' dictum of 'I think, therefore I am' (*cogito ergo sum*), Mill agrees that our understanding of consciousness derives entirely from our own minds.

However, in order to be justified in the belief that other minds exist which are similar to our own, we need to draw parallels between the workings of our minds and the minds of others. If we can recognize certain mental attributes in others that correspond to our own we can infer the existence of other minds similar to our own:

> *I conclude that other human beings have feelings like me, because, first, they have bodies like me, which I know in my own case to be the antecedent condition of feelings; and because, secondly, they exhibit the acts and other outward signs, which in my own case I know to be caused by feelings.*
>
> JOHN STUART MILL, *THE COLLECTED WORKS OF JOHN STUART MILL*, VOLUME IX – 'AN EXAMINATION OF SIR WILLIAM HAMILTON'S PHILOSOPHY' (1865)

Thus, we draw our knowledge, and justification of the existence and workings, of other minds based upon analogy with the understanding of the workings of our own minds. Mill's concept of analogous inference held sway in philosophical circles until the mid-twentieth century and the posthumous publication of Ludwig Wittgenstein's (1889–1951) *Philosophical Investigations* (1953). Wittgenstein's objection to Mill's argument was based upon Mill claiming in his original essay that his conclusions conform 'to the legitimate rules of experimental enquiry':

> *If I say of myself that it is only from my own case that I know what the word 'pain' means – must I not say the same of other people too? And how can I generalize the one case so irresponsibly?*
>
> LUDWIG WITTGENSTEIN,
> *PHILOSOPHICAL INVESTIGATIONS* (1953)

For Wittgenstein, Mill doesn't refute the notion of solipsism but inadvertently endorses it. Using the human concept of pain as an example, Wittgenstein argues that by saying one can deduce that another sentient being is feeling pain because they are behaving in a manner consistent with one's own reactions to pain, is merely to ascribe your understanding of the word pain on to another. It doesn't prove that they feel pain the same way that you do, or vice versa:

> *I can know that others are in pain because they exhibit learned pain behaviour on the same basis that I do, but I cannot know that they* feel *pain to anything like a comparable extent.*
>
> LUDWIG WITTGENSTEIN,
> *PHILOSOPHICAL INVESTIGATIONS* (1953)

Philosophical Investigations is mainly concerned with confusions around the use of language and meaning. Wittgenstein analyses the supposed difference between *public language*, as used in discourse, and the possibility of a *private language* of the mind. Wittgenstein came to the conclusion that all mental operations are linked to our understanding of language, which is socially acquired. Therefore, private language doesn't exist, for in order for it to exist it couldn't be translated by anybody else (otherwise it would become a *public language*).

To return to the question of the extent to which we can know whether other people think and feel the same as us, Wittgenstein would argue that this is only possible through the prism of language and the application of certain criteria. Wittgenstein uses a metaphor of an 'idle wheel' to describe the notion of thoughts that exist independent of their contexts, 'a wheel that can be turned but nothing else moves with it'. Think of moments such as when you are part of a social group talking and somebody says something, expresses a thought, just as you were about to say the same thing. This is because you are engaging in the *public language* of discourse. Although you had the same thought simultaneously, it does not follow that you experienced consciousness together, you just engaged in the language of discourse at the same point in time.

How do we tell the difference between right and wrong?

Differentiating between right and wrong appears to be straightforward when considering questions concerned with an area of philosophy often referred to as *epistemic possibility*. This is the evaluation of propositions according to what we know (or at least, *think* we know) to be true. For instance, we know we must drink water and eat food in order to live because if we deprive ourselves of these essentials we will eventually die. This qualifies as an *epistemic necessity*, something which is true according to our knowledge of the facts of existence. However, observe a small child painting a picture of a landscape and ask them what colour they are going to paint the sky. It would be no surprise if they replied 'blue', but ask the child why and it is likely they will say 'because the sky is blue' and smile at you condescendingly. The child is expressing an *epistemic possibility* – a belief based on what they think they know to be *right* and true according to the limits of their own knowledge and experience. 'Ah', you say slyly, 'but what colour is the sky at night?' The child gives you a withering look and states quite clearly that they are painting the sky during the daytime and if they wanted to paint the sky at night they would paint it purple and blue. 'Not black?' you ask. 'No!' replies the child irritably and explains to you that the sky is never, strictly speaking, black, it just appears black as there isn't enough light to stimulate our colour senses. The child points out that black sky is an *epistemic impossibility* and is therefore wrong, and if you need any further proof go and look at the moody skies in the paintings of El Greco.

The above example draws clear lines between what we believe is right or wrong according to our knowledge and experiences and what we think may be right or wrong according to our perceptions of the available facts. Distinguishing between right and wrong becomes much more complex when it involves moral and ethical issues, actions and judgements. *Deontology* is the area of philosophy that concerns itself with how individuals should behave according to a set of binding rules and principles. What, in any given situation, is the right course to take? *Religious deontology* is in the form of a set of divine commandments derived from sacrosanct texts or other sources that are interpreted as the word of God, such as The Ten Commandments of the Old Testament of the Bible. The word *deontology* is formed from the Ancient Greek word *deon* meaning duty or obligation. *Religious deontology* requires individuals to submit to religious laws and principles such as 'thou shall not kill'. *Secular deontology* (non-religious) is most notably represented by the writings of the German Enlightenment philosopher Immanuel Kant (1724–1804).

In contrast to religious deontological theories, the rules (or maxims) in Kant's deontological theory are founded on the human capacity to reason. Kant's theories also depart from other secular deontological systems such as *utilitarianism* and *consequentialism* in that they question the validity of judging the moral value of an action according to its outcomes. Utilitarians such as its British founder Jeremy Bentham (who published *An Introduction to the Principles of Morals and Legislation* in 1789) and John Stuart Mill (who developed the theory in *Utilitarianism* in 1863), believe that happiness is the highest ideal, the absolute good, and that the moral worth of an action can be measured by its contribution in maximizing the happiness and pleasure for the greatest number of people. Consequentialism is a variant of utilitarianism which states that the final consequence or ultimate end of an action determines its moral validity, regardless of whether the action itself is good or bad. Or, put simply, the end justifies the means.

Kant's deontology refutes the consequence-based view of judging whether an action is right or wrong according to its outcome. For Kant, some actions are always wrong regardless of the end result (and conversely, a wrong action can often result in a favourable outcome, thereby contradicting the rational process). Kant believed that humans, in contrast to animals, have a unique facility for rational thought and it is precisely this ability that compels us to act according to moral laws and codes. Human desires and emotions provide no rational basis for deciding right and wrong, whereas morality, if derived from pure reason, stands autonomously as a framework to guide judgements. Kant referred to this moral code as the *categorical imperative*; that is, the expression of the human will which must be, by its nature, good and just and free from external factors, influences and forces.

The first formulation

Act only according to that maxim whereby you can at the same time will that it should become a universal law without contradiction.

IMMANUEL KANT, *GROUNDWORK OF THE METAPHYSICS OF MORALS* (1785)

The categorical imperative consists of three binding formulations. The first formulation states that moral choices fall into two categories: perfect and imperfect duties. Perfect duties are universal laws that can be applied to any rational human being and are not determined by external conditions and contexts. Imperfect duties are predicated on circumstances, so are open for interpretation and can therefore be disputed (See *The Axe Murderer Dilemma*). Imperfect duties are not constants and are very much of the moment. On the surface, the first categorical imperative appears to be strikingly similar to the Golden Rule or Ethic of Reciprocity, which states that one should 'do unto others as one would have done unto oneself'. However, the Golden Rule requires context in order to be tested and so cannot be considered universal. For example: don't hit another person if you don't want them to hit you back. But what if you are striking out in self-defence?

The second formulation

Act in such a way that you treat humanity, whether in your own person or in the person of any other, never merely as a means to an end but always at the same time as an end. IBID.

The second imperative states that any choice of action, in order to be moral, must itself be considered an end. The human will, if truly autonomous, should recognize the actions and duties of others. To use people as a means to an end, no matter how worthy or appealing the possible outcome may seem, is to deny them their own facility for free will and action. It is therefore important to pursue an outcome that is equal and just for all, not just as a short-term personal objective.

The third formulation

Therefore, every rational being must so act as if he were through his maxim always a legislating member in the universal kingdom of ends. IBID.

The third imperative states that expressions of the human will should be viewed as laws that all should abide by, for if laws are not universal they promote instability and contradictions. This is most apparent in the moral law that it is wrong to lie, regardless of the circumstances, for lying destabilizes truth and trust and if everybody lied nobody would ever trust anybody else. An example of this law of universal ends is the parable of visiting a sick relative or friend. On the way to see your friend you walk across the park and happen upon some pretty wild flowers. You know that your friend loves flowers; however, if everybody picked the flowers there would be none left in the park for people to enjoy in the future. Therefore, although the motive for picking the flowers is one of kindness and consideration, it is morally wrong to do so.

> ❦ Good and evil, rewards and punishment,
> are the only motives to a rational creature. ❧
>
> JOHN LOCKE, *SOME THOUGHTS
> CONCERNING EDUCATION* (1693)

The main problem with applying Kant's deontology to the question of determining right and wrong is the refusal to accept outcomes as a legitimate reason. Although to determine the moral worth of an action solely according to its outcomes has its flaws (see *What is happiness?*), to deny them completely can often seem to contradict common sense.

The Axe Murderer Dilemma

One of Immanuel Kant's most famous tests of his moral philosophy is the example of the madman with the axe. Late one night there is a knock at your door. You open the door and are confronted by a man with an axe demanding to know the whereabouts of a close friend of yours. You know exactly where your friend is (they are hiding under the bed upstairs). Do you tell the axe-wielding psychopath where your friend is hiding or do you lie and send him away to look somewhere else? Most people, without hesitation, would take the second option and lie. Kant believed otherwise and argued that to lie would be to contradict the categorical imperative to always tell the truth, regardless of the outcome. Although once the axe murderer has chopped up your friend it is highly probable he will do the same to you, at least you can die knowing you were morally pure and righteous. If, however, you lie and your lie backfires, then you are morally responsible for the murderous outcomes, because you broke the categorical imperative not to lie in the first place.

The categorical imperative and World War Two

The dilemmas relating to right and wrong and Kant's categorical imperative had a part to play in Germany during World War Two. The anti-Nazi activist and resistance fighter Dietrich Bonhoeffer was a noted scholar of theology. An outspoken opponent of the Third Reich, Bonhoeffer was imprisoned and executed for his part in various plots to assassinate Adolf Hitler. Bonhoeffer's surviving works, particularly his letters and sermons, reveal a man grappling with the moral question of whether it is acceptable to kill one person in order to save the lives of millions, if killing in itself is morally wrong. Bonhoeffer may have finally decided it was, under such extreme circumstances, permissible, although not without reservations, as the following extract from his unfinished work on morality and ethics illustrates:

When a man takes guilt upon himself in responsibility, he imputes his guilt to himself and no one else. He answers for it … Before other men he is justified by dire necessity; before himself he is acquitted by his conscience, but before God he hopes only for grace.

Kant's categorical imperative also became a point of contention during the trial of the Holocaust administrator Adolf Eichmann. The defence Eichmann used against the multiple charges of crimes against humanity was that he was following orders and that he was not personally responsible for issuing the orders, merely for implementing them. In the course of the trial, Eichmann deployed various tactics to justify his position, one of which was to attempt to invoke Kant's categorical imperative and draw the prosecution into a philosophical debate about moral responsibility. Eichmann claimed to be an avid follower of Kant's universal view of morality but was unable to act with moral purity due to higher powers restricting his capacity for free will. The prosecution refused to accept Eichmann's pretentious distortion of Kant's deontology and he was found guilty and executed in Jerusalem in 1962.

Immanuel Kant (1724–1804)

Immanuel Kant was born in 1724 in the Prussian city of Königsberg (now part of Russia). An avid scholar with an insatiable thirst for knowledge, Kant spent virtually his entire life in his home city, studying and teaching at the university. Best known for his work in the field of moral philosophy and ethics, Kant was also a highly skilled scientist who made several key discoveries in mathematics, astrophysics and the natural sciences. Although Kant lectured on anthropology, it is only recently that his work in this field has come to be revered. In 1997 Kant's lectures on anthropology were published for the first time in Germany, almost two centuries after his death

In common with many of his contemporaries, Kant's published works about the nature of reality and free will were widely criticized and disputed during his lifetime but have had a profound influence on the development of Western thought. Kant's most notable works on morality and ethics are *Groundwork of the Metaphysics of Morals* (1785), *The Critique of Practical Reason* (1788) and *Metaphysics of Morals* (1798).

What is
bad faith?

Existentialism is a philosophical movement that became prominent in post-war France and is closely associated with the writings of John Paul Sartre (1905–1980) and Albert Camus (1913–1960). The central tenet of existentialism is to foreground the distinctiveness and isolation of individual human experience. Our personal, lived experience, our own existence, is what defines us as individuals. Sartre makes a clear distinction between existence on one hand and essence on the other, giving primacy to the former. Existentialism places considerable stress on individual freedom of choice and responsibility. This freedom entails considering the consequences of one's actions and how they affect the development of our personality and sense of self. How an individual acts is the defining characteristic of our existence. For example, if one chooses to commit brutal and malicious acts, one is positioning oneself as a brutal and malicious person and must take responsibility for the consequences of such actions. If, on the other hand, one chooses to do kind and thoughtful acts, one is positioning oneself as a kind and thoughtful person. An individual is intrinsically neither good nor bad:

they define themselves through their personal choice of action.

Jean Paul Sartre first became interested in philosophy after encountering Henri Bergson's essay 'Time and Free Will' which formed part of Bergson's doctoral thesis first published in 1889. Sartre studied philosophy in his native Paris at the École Normale Supérieure, and became particularly interested in the ideas of the Dane Søren Kierkegaard (1813–1855), and the Germans Edmund Husserl (1859–1938) and Martin Heidegger (1889–1976). In 1929 Sartre met Simone de Beauvoir, a student at the Sorbonne, and the pair became lifelong companions. Although both came from 'bourgeois' families, Sartre and de Beauvoir held strong political beliefs which inform their writings on the nature of society and the place of the individual.

The key to Sartre's philosophy is the tension and conflict between the oppressive forces of conformity that attempt to define individuals into social groups and the authenticity which Sartre saw as essential to self-determination. In order to achieve an authentic mode of existence, an individual must accept responsibility for all the actions that they freely choose. This total freedom to choose is not without its dangers and Sartre recognized that the burden of making the right choice in any given situation can often give rise to a state of existential anguish. By making false choices – life decisions based on imposed ideologies and objective norms – human beings exist inauthentically and embody what Sartre describes as *bad faith*. The concept of bad faith in existentialism echoes the Marxist idea of false consciousness; that is, the processes – material, institutional and ideological – through which capitalist societies control and manipulate the proletariat. Sartre's bad faith relates more explicitly to individual choice. Ideology, for Sartre, acts almost exclusively as a mystification of individuals' capacity for free thought and therefore diminishes the opportunity of autonomous and meaningful action.

To live in bad faith is to deny that we are free and responsible for what we are and do, when in fact the very nature of existence determines that we are. Bad faith is denial of free will on the grounds that we, like everything in the universe, are causally determined and thus we have no true freedom as we are merely victims of circumstance. In order to live an authentic existence, Sartre suggested that individuals should be true to their own beliefs and ideas. This entails ascribing meaning to our choices and actions, and to defy the external imposition of meaning. The value of life is measured only by the beliefs each individual freely chooses to apply. The argument that humans are victims of pre-determined fate and subject to forces over which we have no control, such as class, race, gender and religion, is to live according to bad faith.

❝ Man first of all exists, encounters
himself, surges up in the world – and
defines himself afterwards. ❞

JOHN PAUL SARTRE, 'EXISTENTIALISM
IS A HUMANISM' (1946)

Sartre first discussed bad faith in his 1943 book *Being
and Nothingness*. Sartre had read Martin Heidegger's
Being and Time (1927) whilst a prisoner of war, and
Heidegger's ideas about 'nothing' (see also *Why is there
something rather than nothing?*) are a clear influence on
his thought. Sartre borrows Heidegger's term 'facticity'
to describe the evident facts of an individual's existence
and the facts that are assumed to constitute their identity
(birth, gender, religion, geographical location, the
inevitability of death), and suggests that these elements
are obstructions to true freedom, responsibility
and authenticity. For example, if a person is born in
Germany it is highly likely they will grow up speaking
German. If, however, they go to live in France and
choose to speak exclusively French for the rest of their
life they are denying the facticity of their language of
birth. This is an example of what Sartre terms 'negation',
and it is through negation (by embracing nothingness)
that individuals can overcome the adversity of their
facticity. By negation or the conscious contemplation

of 'nothingness' in our everyday lived experience, we can subvert facticity into 'nothing', and ascribe our own meanings to our actions.

'You don't arrest Voltaire'

The emphasis on negation and rejecting conformity in Sartre's philosophy provided the countercultural movements in France with an intellectual and philosophical backbone in the 1960s and 70s. Alongside his academic and literary writings, Sartre was a lifelong political activist. A staunch Marxist (although he never joined the Communist Party), Sartre spoke out against French colonial rule in Algeria, vehemently opposed the Vietnam War and visited Fidel Castro and Che Guevara in Cuba. He was also a prominent figurehead for the student movement in Paris during the late 1960s and was arrested during the riots of May 1968 for civil disorder. President Charles de Gaulle intervened and issued Sartre with a pardon on the grounds that 'You don't arrest Voltaire'.

Is the glass half full or half empty?

This classic dilemma is a mainstay of popular psychology, self-improvement books and life-coaching. Bookshop shelves are stacked high with titles such as *How to Be a Success in Business* or *25 Paths to Follow to Reach Your Ideal Life Destination* and almost all of them will at some point discuss the concept of 'positive visualization'. The question 'is the glass half full or half empty?' is central to positive visualization and hinges on the premise that a person who views the metaphorical glass as half empty is, by natural inclination, a pessimist, and a person who views the glass as half full has a more optimistic outlook on the world.

It isn't hard to imagine Socrates gathering his pupils beneath the colonnades in the market squares of ancient Athens and exhorting them to discuss whether his carafe of wine was half full or half empty. However, the framing of the question is relatively modern. Nonetheless, the implications of adopting an optimistic or a pessimistic philosophy on human life and society have been analysed and discussed by philosophers throughout history.

Stoicism in Ancient Greece and Rome

Many philosophers have explored the links between happiness and the fulfilment of human needs and desires. The Ancient Greek (and later Roman) philosophy of *stoicism* adopted an interesting approach to happiness, which on the face of it could be said to reflect 'a half empty' point of view but on closer inspection is deeper and more complex than just assuming the worst.

The school of philosophy known as Stoicism was founded by the Athenian street teacher Zeno of Citium around 300 BCE. Zeno's ideas gained widespread popularity through adoption by noted Roman writers, philosophers and scholars such as Seneca the Younger, Epictetus and the warrior and philosopher Emperor Marcus Aurelius. The basic tenet of Stoic philosophy is to adopt virtues that are at one with the natural order of things: the cosmic principle that the Greeks named *logos*. Each of us faces negative and destructive elements and emotions, be they self-generated or external, over which we have no direct influence or control. The Stoics recommend that we must develop a state of tranquillity and calm. This state of at-one-ness with the universe, which the Stoics describe as 'pure virtue', can be achieved by closely examining the negative factors external to oneself, and embracing a glass half-empty perspective.

> *Be like a rocky promontory against which the restless surf continually pounds; it stands fast while the churning sea is lulled to sleep at its feet. I hear you say, 'How unlucky that this should happen to me!' Not at all! Say instead, 'How lucky that I am not broken by what has happened and am not afraid of what is about to happen. The same blow might have struck anyone, but not many would have absorbed it without capitulation or complaint.'*
>
> MARCUS AURELIUS, **MEDITATIONS** (*c.* 170–180)

Noisy neighbours

Negative situations external to ourselves provoke anger, envy, anxiety and pain, or so we let ourselves believe. Take the noisy neighbours who have recently moved in next door. The noise from the raucous parties at weekends, the rubbish bags strewn all over the pavements outside, the perceived indifference and lack of consideration for other people, are causing extreme irritation and distress. It's no wonder one feels angry, put upon and unwittingly oppressed. And yet, Stoics would say, are any of the causes for these negative emotions being provoked internally actually negative in themselves? The sound of young people enjoying themselves shouldn't be a cause for anger, neither should the fact that our new neighbours don't conform to our own exacting standards of cleanliness. And to assume that our interpretation of their behaviour is evidence that they lack consideration and compassion for others is arrogant – and rather pious.

The point the Stoics would make about the noisy neighbours is that nothing outside our own minds can be defined as either positive or negative; what causes distress are the beliefs and opinions we have of a situation beyond our direct control. We could petition the local powers-that-be for an anti-social behaviour order, or, to take the matter to extremes, confront our neighbours with threats of physical violence. For the Stoics, either of these actions would constitute a disaster, as it would move us ever further away from a state of tranquillity within the natural order of the universe and cause us ever-increasing mental and emotional turmoil.

Philosophical optimism versus philosophical pessimism

Where the Stoics took an individual view of the glass half full or half empty question, two notable German philosophers adopted a more universal perspective by examining the nature of the world around us in its entirety. The main proponent of philosophical optimism was the seventeenth-century German polymath Gottfried Wilhelm Leibniz (1646–1716). Leibniz wrote important works on a wide range of subjects from mathematics, physics and logic to politics and philosophy, with perhaps his most telling contribution being the development (along with Sir Isaac Newton) of infinitesimal calculus in mathematical analysis.

Leibniz's major philosophical work was *Théodicée* (*Theodicy*, 1710), essentially a long and reasoned evaluation of the problem of how a good God could possibly create a bad world full of evil and suffering. Leibniz concluded that when all possible elements are taken into consideration, the world as God created is the best He could possibly have created, for if we are to accept the grounding premise that God is omnipotent (all-seeing) and omnibenevolent (all-good) then it does not follow that such a God could produce something deliberately bad. Leibniz argues that the imperfections of the world are part of its overall design and a manifestation of its enduring beauty, by pointing to music and how some of the most beautiful music is created through the dissonance of elements, combined into a coherent whole. Therefore, according to Leibniz: 'We live in the best of all possible worlds'.

> 6 An optimist is a person who sees a green light everywhere, while a pessimist sees only the red stoplight. The truly wise person is colour blind. 9
>
> ALBERT SCHWEITZER, (1875–1965)

On the other side of the fence, philosophical pessimism was outlined by Arthur Schopenhauer (1788–1860) most notably in his text *The World as Will and Representation* (1818). In Schopenhauer's world, the glass is virtually empty, taking as he did the guiding principle that humans are born to suffer. Suffering occurs because of a pervasive restlessness in human consciousness provoked by constant needs and desires, for reasons of survival, avoidance of discomfort and relief of boredom.

Schopenhauer defines this inner striving and its incumbent restlessness as the 'will to live', which is endless. The need for food and shelter, security and safety from malign elements, sexuality and the need to procreate, are all manifestations of this *will*, with reason merely a process of justifying our base needs and desires. By drawing comparisons between human life and animals in the natural world, Schopenhauer asserted that the reproductive cycle was a pointless process that was doomed to either continue indefinitely (eternal suffering through the will to live) or to ultimately be brought to an end by extinction through lack of the sustainable resources needed to make continued life possible. Thus human life has two choices, either to pointlessly and endlessly continue its cycle of suffering or face extinction.

�֍

Schopenhauer's breakfast

Schopenhauer maintained throughout his professional life a bitter rivalry with Germany's other great philosopher of the early nineteenth century, Georg Wilhelm Friedrich Hegel (1770–1831). This rivalry began with an intellectual disagreement over Hegel's concept of the *zeitgeist* – the collective consciousness that drives the movement and momentum in society – but quickly spiralled into verbal abuse and name-calling. In 1819 Schopenhauer accepted his first and only academic seat at the University of Berlin simply because Hegel also had a chair there. In a rather childish attempt to provoke a popularity competition,

Schopenhauer deliberately scheduled his lectures to coincide with Hegel's. His plan backfired, however, as Hegel proved to be far more popular among the discerning student intelligentsia. Schopenhauer left the university after less than a year in the post.

Riddled with bitterness and a persecution complex that the German academic establishment were deliberately suppressing his works, Schopenhauer withdrew from public life and spent the last two decades of his life living alone with his pet poodles in Frankfurt. The essays and notes he produced during his latter years were published posthumously and are characterized by a nihilistic gloominess which was to prove a big influence on the philosophy of Friedrich Nietzsche. In one memorable essay on the nature of growing old, collected in the posthumous collection *Senilia*, Schopenhauer advises that everyone should swallow a live toad for their daily breakfast as a means of ensuring that they won't have to suffer an experience quite as dispiriting again for the rest of the day.

What is
happiness?

Philosophical writing on the subject of happiness can be broadly split into two strands. On one side is a hedonistic view of happiness as the pursuit of personal pleasure, or the promotion of pleasure as an intrinsic good in opposition to sorrow and pain. The other philosophical view of happiness relates to notions of personal virtue and ethics and, more practically, the question of how to live a happy life.

The hedonistic approach to happiness was first postulated by Aristippus of Cyrene (435–356 BCE), a former student of Socrates. Aristippus, in common with other Greek philosophers, engaged with the question of where to find the value of fulfilment in human thoughts and actions. The pleasure of the senses was paramount for Aristippus in relation to happiness and should be viewed as an end in itself and not a means to an end. Aristippus rejected the idea of deferring pleasures that were available in the present as a means of working towards some future planned ideal and taught that pleasures should always be indulged as and when opportunities present themselves. Diogenes Laërtius, author of the third-century chronicle *Lives of the Great Philosophers*, presents a portrait of Aristippus as a man driven by his desires, which he indulged at every possible occasion. However, the Roman lyric poet Horace describes the philosophy of Aristippus as not a matter of simple, reckless, hedonistic abandon but of adapting circumstances to one's own ends, as opposed to having to compromise to circumstances. The placing of pleasure at the centre of analysing happiness was developed later by the philosopher Epicurus (341–271 BCE), who, although often considered a hedonist, preached a more moderate and ethical approach (see *Is too much better than not enough?*).

The second strand of thinking about happiness concerns how to live a happy life and its relation to notions of well-being and contentment, as opposed to fleeting moments of pleasure and joy. Invariably, the problem here is one of the extent to which the pursuit of personal well-being impacts upon personal virtues. Aristotle was one of the first philosophers to approach and analyse the ethics of happiness.

Aristotle (384–322 BCE) remains a towering figure in the history of human thought. He made valuable contributions to an astonishing range of disciplines, including physics, metaphysics, poetry, theatre, music, logic, rhetoric, linguistics, politics and government, ethics, biology and zoology (his method of categorizing species is still used to this day). Aristotle's main contribution to the field of philosophy was in the area of formal logic and deductive reasoning. The formulations of syllogisms or a three-step argument was central to Aristotle's methodology. In short, a syllogism consists of two premises followed by a proposition. In order for a proposition to be viable, the two preceeding premises must be valid and true. Aristotle's famous example is as follows:

> *All men are mortal.*
> *Socrates is a man.*
> *Therefore Socrates is mortal.*

Aristotle's writings on happiness are contained on a set of scrolls transcribed from his teachings at The Lyceum, an academy of arts and sciences he founded in Athens. The scrolls, collectively known as the *Nicomachean Ethics* (350 BCE), address the question of what constitutes a good and virtuous life. Aristotle equates the concept of happiness with the Greek word *eudaimonia*, although this is not happiness in an abstract or hedonistic sense, but rather 'excellence' and 'well-being'. To live well, then, is to aim at doing good or the best one can, for every human activity has an outcome or cause, the good at which it aims to achieve. If humans strive to be happy, the highest good should be the aim of all actions, not a means to an end, but an end in itself.

❝ Happiness is when what you think, what you say and what you do are in harmony. ❞

MAHATMA GANDHI (1869–1948)

Aristotle saw the pursuit of happiness as 'being a realization and perfect practice of virtue', which could be achieved by applying reason and intellect to control their desires. The satisfaction of desires and the acquisition of material goods are less important than the achievement of virtue. A happy person will apply conformity and moderation to achieve a natural and appropriate balance between reason and desire. Virtue itself should be its own reward as true happiness can be attained only through the cultivation of the virtues that make a human life complete. Aristotle also points out that the exercise of perfect virtue should be consistent throughout a person's life: 'to be happy takes a complete lifetime, for one swallow does not make spring.'

Aristotle's *Nicomachean Ethics* had a profound influence on the development of Christian theology throughout the Middle Ages. St Augustine of Hippo studied Aristotle and admired his works and St Thomas Aquinas produced several important studies of Aristotle's thought, particularly through Aquinas' project to synthesize Aristotle's notion of pure virtue with Catholic doctrines concerning cardinal virtues.

Aristotle's works were also highly revered in early Islamic philosophy, where Aristotle is often referred to as 'The First Teacher'.

> *The unexamined life is not worth living.*
>
> SOCRATES (*c.* 469–399 BC)

What is
freedom?

Debates about the nature of concepts such as freedom
and liberty are central to political philosophy and
the development of political systems and ideologies.
Plato's *Republic* (*c*. 380 BCE) is considered to be one of
the earliest major works dedicated to analysing how
political systems work and evaluating ideas of justice,
freedom and truth in human society. In modern Western
societies it is generally held that liberal democracy,
'government of the people by the people and for the
people', is the most desirable and justifiable political
system. The central tenets of democracy are freedom
and equality. Democracy provides freedom for people
to self-govern in their own collective interests, either
directly, or by appointed or elected representatives. In
Republic Plato confronts two essential elements of the
democracy practised in Ancient Greece, freedom and
equality, in order to evaluate democracy as a viable
political model. Although Plato considers freedom,
in essence, to be a true and pure value, there are
dangers inherent if freedom is granted as the right to
do whatever one likes, unrestricted by responsibility
or guidance. Plato suggests that such a free-for-all

approach encourages instability and confusion at best and downright anarchy and lawlessness at worst. Turning his attention to equality, Plato notes that true equality is linked to equality of opportunity and the principle that everyone has the right and equal capacity to rule. However, the danger of this standard of equality is that it could encourage individuals who are motivated by a thirst for power, influence and personal gain at the expense of the common good. A fully functioning democracy needs to be mindful of the dangers of malign influences from demagogues and dictators and requires leaders with enlightened values. Plato suggests that philosophers are ideally placed to lead people, as they are able to rationally balance conflicting influences and desires within society as a whole. However, by granting them executive power to safeguard against the excesses of tyranny, individual and personal freedom is restricted. This therefore brings up a paradoxical question concerning a definition of freedom: to what extent are we free from external controls stopping us from doing whatever we choose and to what extent do we have internal controls to command our own destiny?

The philosopher Isaiah Berlin (1909–1997) proposed that there are two distinct types of freedom: positive freedom and negative freedom. Negative freedom is characterized by *freedom from* forces restricting individual subjects doing whatever they desire and is concerned with the absence of external obstacles to freedom. Positive freedom, on the other hand, is characterized by *capacity to* be free and is concerned with the presence of factors such as self-control and self-mastery in the pursuit of personal freedom. Berlin posited two questions key to understanding the distinction between his two concepts:

> *What is the area within which the subject –*
> *a person or group of persons – is or should*
> *be left to do or be what he is able to do or*
> *be, without interference by other persons?*
> *(Negative freedom.)*
>
> *What, or who, is the source of control*
> *or interference that can determine someone*
> *to do, or be, this rather than that? (Positive*
> *freedom.)*
>
> ISAIAH BERLIN, *TWO CONCEPTS OF LIBERTY* (1958)

The difference between our positive and negative freedoms can be established by looking at a simple, everyday example:

A)   I would like to go on holiday to Hawaii. In terms of my negative freedom, I can go to Hawaii if nobody puts any obstacles in my way to actively prevent me from doing so. However, if I have a criminal conviction that prevents me from being granted an entrance visa to the USA, for example, my negative freedom has been affected by an external force.

B) I would like to go on holiday to Hawaii. Unfortunately, I suffer from acute angina and so I am unable to manage long-haul flights without putting my health at serious risk. The airline aren't stopping me from buying a plane ticket and, although my doctor has said it isn't a good idea, he can't prevent me from running the risk of travelling, so my negative freedom isn't impinged upon by external forces. However, because I lack the *capacity to* go to Hawaii because of ill health, my positive freedom has been nullified.

In example A), hypothetically, my negative freedom could be restricted by the conditions of entry to the United States. These conditions have been applied by the state, presumably to protect its citizens from undesirable influences, so state intervention in this instance appears justifiable. On the other hand, what if my freedom of movement was restricted on other grounds, such as my ethnic background or political affiliations? Would state intervention and the application of negative freedom be permissible in such circumstances? In example B) my positive freedom could be exercised through the creation of a certain state of affairs conducive to developing my capacity to self-determination. The state could provide free and available health care to help me manage my angina effectively. The airline could put in place medical assistance to ensure my safety during the journey. In this sense, in order for positive freedom to be put into effect, a particular social environment is required. Positive freedom therefore requires the formation of a community with collective ideals.

Jean-Jacques Rousseau's (1712–1778) concept of the 'general will' can be seen as an attempt to articulate an ideology of positive freedom.

> *Man is born free, and everywhere he is in chains. Those who think themselves the masters of others are indeed greater slaves than they.*
>
> JEAN-JACQUES ROUSSEAU, *THE SOCIAL CONTRACT* (1762)

For Rousseau, there are two types of freedom: personal freedom and social freedom. Personal freedom derives from humans' basic instincts, natural selfishness and the imposition of conditions that force individual people to be in competition and conflict with each other in a battle for survival.

Social freedom provides an alternative whereby an individual enters into a social contract and submits to the desires of the *general will* of a community or collective. This promotes a view of society in which every individual acts as a stakeholder and is free to participate in the democratic process. In order for a social contract to work, Rousseau states that personal freedom, individual desires and motivations need to be subjugated to the general will.

> ❝ If liberty means anything at all,
> it means the right to tell people
> what they do not want to hear. ❞
> GEORGE ORWELL, *ANIMAL FARM* (1945)

Concepts of positive and negative freedom and personal and social freedom provide the basis for key debates in modern political theory. Advocates of negative freedom argue that a certain amount of state intervention is permissible in order to safeguard essential liberties such as freedom of movement, freedom of association and freedom to practise a religion. Advocates of positive freedom take the view that the state should intervene to create the conditions to allow individuals to flourish and be self-sufficient in achieving their goals. In essence, the arguments for and against both positive and negative freedom relate to determining the limits of acceptable state interventions or controls and, more fundamentally, establishing how human society should be organized.

❝ Good and evil, rewards and punishment, are the only motives to a rational creature. ❞

JOHN LOCKE (1632–1704)

If there are gods, why do they allow suffering?

Philosophical attempts to reconcile the existence of an omnipotent (all-seeing) and omnibenevolent (all-loving) god, or gods, with a world riddled with pain and suffering has centred on the rhetorical use of *theodicy*. The term theodicy derives from the Greek word *Theos* meaning God, and *dikē*, which roughly translates as 'justification for', hence, 'justification for God'. The term was first used by the German philosopher Gottfried Wilhelm Leibniz (1646–1716 AD) in his work *Théodicée* (1710). Leibniz's central concern was with rationalizing the existence of evil in the world. Evil, in this sense, is not restricted to the Christian concepts of evil and sin, but also includes human pain and suffering. Leibniz was a highly skilled mathematician who some scholars believe may have developed calculus before its historical discovery by Sir Isaac Newton. Through his grounding in mathematics and formal logic, Leibniz's theoretical philosophy takes a deterministic approach, that is, that everything that occurs is the result of pre-determined conditions.

Leibniz bases his theodicy on the premise that God is all-powerful and the source of all that is good in the world. As God created the world, he must have created it as perfectly as possible, for it is not logical that an all-powerful God would deliberately create an inferior, imperfect world. This led to Leibniz's famed conclusion that we live 'in the best of all possible worlds' (see also *Is the glass half full or half empty?*).

❛ About suffering they were never wrong,
The old Masters: how well they understood
Its human position: how it takes place
While someone else is eating or opening a
window or just walking dully along… ❜

W. H. AUDEN, *MUSÉE DES BEAUX ARTS* (1938)

The sceptical counterargument to Leibniz's best of all worlds theory is that imperfections are visible through the existence of evil and suffering, which are presumably permitted by God by their very existence. Leibniz responds that God is possessed of infinite wisdom but that his creations (humans) are not, and are limited by their abilities in thought and action (human will) to change pre-determined conditions.

This limitation in the freedom of the human will has led to false beliefs and erroneous actions, which in turn have led to suffering and pain. In short, it is humans who inflict misery and suffering upon each other, not God, who acts merely as an arbiter, for the forces of good can only become apparent to the human mind by necessary contrast with the forces of evil and pain. In forbearing suffering, human beings will learn from their false beliefs and decisions and step 'into the light of righteous truth'.

Leibniz's 'best of all possible worlds' theory found its most vociferous opponent in the works of the French writer and philosopher François-Marie Arouet, better known by his pen name Voltaire (1694–1778). A prolific writer and philosopher, Voltaire amassed a vast oeuvre including plays, poetry, novels, essays, historical and scientific works, over 21,000 letters and more than two thousand books and pamphlets.

Candide (1759) is Voltaire's best-known work, a picaresque novel constructed around a sustained and withering attack on the philosophy of Leibniz, ironically satirizing Leibniz's particular brand of philosophical and moral optimism. Voltaire's main contention seems to be that there is too much observable evil and suffering in the world and this is disproportionate to the amount of observable good. Voltaire finds Leibniz guilty of blind optimism (*The Optimist* is the subtitle of the novel) and Voltaire creates Dr Pangloss, an unreserved disciple of Leibniz's philosophy, as a vehicle to deride philosophical optimism. The eponymous anti-hero, Candide, is placed under the tutelage of the arrogant and buffoonish Pangloss, who constantly expounds his doctrine that everything has a purpose and things happen 'for the best'. Throughout the novel, the eponymous hero lurches from one catastrophe to the next, enduring wars, earthquakes and shipwrecks along the way. Many of these calamities are rationalized by Pangloss, using Leibniz's formula that evil is a necessary consequence for greater good. Much of Pangloss's logic is laughable, such as claiming that syphilis, allegedly brought to Europe by Columbus, was a good thing because Columbus also discovered chocolate, or that the Lisbon earthquake that claimed 30,000 lives was 'all for the best'. In an ironic twist, however, the vain and pretentious Pangloss lectures a member of the Portuguese Inquisition on his philosophical system and is promptly charged with heresy and executed.

Although Voltaire's satirical attacks against Leibniz's and Pangloss's optimism seem, on the surface, to promote a gloomy and cynical view of the world and human nature, Voltaire was not an atheist. A key figure in the European Enlightenment, Voltaire held the belief that humans could find moral virtue through reason, and that reason allied to the observation of the natural world was adequate to determine the existence of God. The Lisbon earthquake seemed to have a big effect on Voltaire's philosophy, leading him to believe that humans can and should be able to make a better world for themselves and for future generations. In this respect, Voltaire saw Leibniz's 'best of all possible worlds' as an obstacle to progress and change and a justification for maintaining the status quo.

The freedom of speech defence Voltaire never made

Voltaire's *Dictionnaire Philosophique* (1764) is considered his major contribution to philosophy but is not a dictionary in the conventional sense but a large miscellaneous collection of essays and pamphlets on whatever subjects took his fancy. One notable aspect of Voltaire's philosophical writing was a tendency towards constructing impassioned polemical arguments built around the use of aphorisms. Two of Voltaire's most memorable aphorisms, 'Optimism is the madness of insisting all is well when we are miserable' or 'Every man is guilty of all the good he did not do', are self-consciously literary in style, displaying the often paradoxical nature of Voltaire's thought, and had considerable influence upon later writers such as Oscar Wilde. The quote most often attributed to Voltaire is on the subject of freedom of speech: 'I disapprove of what you say, but I will defend to the death your right to say it.' Ironically, the quote does not appear in any of Voltaire's collected letters or any other writings for that matter but derives from an apocryphal story in English writer Evelyn Beatrice Hall's 1906 biography of Voltaire, *The Friends of Voltaire*.

Do animals have rights?

The question of the extent to which animals have rights may seem to be a modern philosophical debate, one born from liberal democracies and a natural progression from concepts of human rights, liberty and freedom. However, arguments for and against animal rights have engaged thinkers as diverse as Plutarch, Descartes and Nietzsche throughout the history of philosophy. The Ancient Greek scholar Plutarch (46–120 CE), addressed the ethical issues of rearing animals for food in his essay 'On Eating Flesh'. Plutarch is best known for his detailed biographies of Greek and Roman philosophers and statesmen contained in his series of works *Parallel Lives*, and as a chronicler of classical society. In addition to his contribution to history, Plutarch was also an avid essayist who wrote polemical works on a vast range of subjects, from the correct way to study poetry and philosophy to marriage guidance counselling and parenting skills. These essays are collectively known as the *Moralia*, which includes Plutarch's famous diatribe on animal rights.

In 'On Eating Flesh', Plutarch's argument against eating meat is two-fold. Firstly, Plutarch takes issue with the commonly held idea that human beings are naturally carnivorous. The human body, Plutarch argues, is not designed to consume flesh. Our mouths and the arrangement of our teeth and other physical attributes do not suggest an animal for whom hunting, killing and devouring animals is a biological necessity. Furthermore, Plutarch points out the hypocrisy in human meat-eating by arguing that other carnivores, who kill through necessity, eat the flesh whilst it is still warm or 'as it lies', whereas human beings cure and prepare meat for consumption 'so that the palate may be deceived and accept what is foreign to it'. Plutarch challenges meat eaters to prove they are true carnivores by killing in a noble fashion with their bare hands without the use of weapons. Plutarch's second argument centres on the ethical and spiritual question of the rights and wrongs of eating meat. Plutarch dismisses the notion that animals lack a soul or consciousness and points to much animal behaviour that shows intelligence and sentience:

> *For the sake of some little mouthful of flesh, we deprive a soul of the sun and light ... And then we fancy that the voices it utters and screams forth to us are nothing else but certain inarticulate sounds and noises, and not the entreaties of each of them.*
>
> PLUTARCH, 'ON EATING FLESH' (c. 100 CE)

Moreover, Plutarch argues the cruelty by which meat is acquired brutalizes the human character, which not only makes it callous to the suffering of non-human animals but, by legitimizing brutality, encourages similar behaviour towards other human beings. Plutarch's arguments had a considerable effect on Greek intellectual circles, most notably on the neo-Platonist school of philosophers founded by Plotinus and his pupil Porphyry (234–305 CE), who were both dedicated vegans.

The French Enlightenment philosopher René Descartes (1596–1650) provided the counter position to the question of the extent to which animals have rights in his *Discourse on the Method* (1657). Descartes argued that although animals appear to exhibit intelligence, in fact their behaviour is instinctive and reflexive and wholly determined by simple sensations. An injured dog in the street may whimper and cry out, thereby demonstrating the capacity to feel pain, but this is an impulse that the animal isn't capable of rationalizing or articulating through creative thought and language. Animals are certainly conscious of pain, but lack the capacity for self-conscious or coherent thought regarding the concept of pain, its nature and its consequences. Descartes coined the phrase *bête machine* to liken the responses of animals to certain stimuli as equivalent to that of a malfunctioning machine (although Descartes concedes that *animal machines* are far superior in their construction than man-made machines, by virtue of having been created by God).

> 6 He who abstains from anything animate ... will be much more careful not to injure those of his own species. For he who loves the genus will not hate any species of animals. 9

PORPHYRY (234–305 CE),
ON ABSTINENCE FROM ANIMAL FOOD

The principle objection to Descartes' position concerns the notion of suffering. Many people find images and examples of animal cruelty intolerable, barbarous and uncivilized. The contemporary Australian philosopher Peter Singer (born 1946) argues that to distinguish between human suffering on one hand and the suffering of animals on the other, betrays a failure to fully comprehend what it is about the nature of cruelty, prejudice and oppression that is so morally indefensible in the first place. Singer points out that Descartes' argument ranks access to equality on the basis of perceived intelligence and that to make such an arbitrary distinction echoes the position adopted by slave traders and white supremacists. Singer argues that suffering, in and of itself, is wrong, regardless of who or what is experiencing pain.

If a being suffers, there can be no moral justification for refusing to take that suffering into consideration. No matter what the nature of the being, the principle of equality requires that its suffering be counted equally with the like suffering – in so far as rough comparisons can be made – of any other being.

PETER SINGER, ***PRACTICAL ETHICS*** (1979)

What is time?

The question of the nature of time, its objectivity or subjectivity (whether time exists outside of our immediate perception of it) is a problem that has occupied thinkers since antiquity. Plato wrote in his dialogue *Timaeus* (*c.* 360 BCE): 'Time is the moving image of eternity'. Plato's project was to outline what he believed to be the essential elements that make up the cosmos or universe, and he equates time with the movement of these aspects. Time, for Plato, is eternal and constant, just as the universe is designed to be eternal and constant.

Aristotle further expanded upon Plato's view of time as movement by analysing the relationship between movement and change. For Aristotle, where there is development or movement, there is time. This idea is predicated on the notion that everything that comes in to being, or conversely, ceases to be, exists in time. Change occurs because of time, without time there is no change.

But what exactly is our perception of time? When we think or speak of time it is usually in relation to present time, commonly exemplified by someone asking us 'what time is it?' Aristotle argues that the essence of time is *the now*, the present temporal instant that constitutes immediate experience. However, this seems to contradict Aristotle's view of time as movement and change, as we know that time cannot be static. Time is therefore not only the present 'now', but also the movement between time passed and time not yet occurred.

Aristotle seems to be suggesting therefore that we have no perception of time as an object, but we perceive changes or events *in* time. We do not perceive events only in isolation, but also their sequential relations to one another. This is a similar set of thought processes, in a sense, to perceiving different relations between separate objects. We perceive events in a linear sequence with one following another, for example, night following day. But this presents a paradox. If, as Aristotle asserts, what we perceive in relation to time we perceive as *the present and occurring now*, can we perceive a relationship between two events without also perceiving the events themselves? Or, put another way, in order to perceive both events as now we would need to perceive them both simultaneously, and not in linear sequence after all. In short, when we perceive night as following day we have ceased to perceive day and merely committed it to memory as recent time passed. This seems to suggest that time is a framework for ordering experience.

> ❝ It is utterly beyond our power to measure the changes of things by time ... time is an abstraction at which we arrive through the changes of things. ❞

ERNST MACH, *THE SCIENCE OF MECHANICS* (1893)

At the core of philosophical analysis of the nature of time lies a debate between two opposing schools of thought: on one hand *relationism* and on the other *absolutism*.

The relationist view, as endorsed by Aristotle and Leibniz, states that time cannot exist outside of the events and changes that occur in time, time is a system of temporal relations between things and events. This viewpoint suggests that it is impossible to perceive time without perceiving changes in these temporal relations. The epistemological argument here echoes the argument about the (non) existence of nothing (see *Why is there something rather than nothing?*). It is logically impossible to perceive a period of empty time where nothing occurs.

The absolutist view, as endorsed by Plato and scientists such as Isaac Newton, takes a metaphorical approach. Time, for absolutists, is like a giant, infinite empty filing cabinet into which events and objects and entities are placed and ordered. The filing cabinet exists regardless of what (if anything at all) is placed inside it.

Immanuel Kant in his *Critique of Pure Reason* (1781), developed the absolutism versus relationism argument by equating our conception of time with a form of intuition, or subjective reality. Kant believed that our understanding of time is *a priori* knowledge (something that is innate). Thus, for Kant, time and space cannot exist independently of the mind; rather they are the workings of the mind itself (that is, intuitions). Kant used the term *noumenon* to describe things *as they are* and distinct from *as they may appear*. It is through our intuitions that we are able to translate *noumenon* into comprehendible phenomenon such as time.

�֎

Time without change – a thought experiment

In an attempt to challenge the Aristotelian view that time cannot be perceived without movement or change, American philosopher Sydney Shoemaker constructed the following hypothesis in 1969. Shoemaker described a parallel world divided into three zones and labelled them Zone 1, Zone 2 and Zone 3.

In Zone 1 something peculiar occurs every two years; there is a period of one hour where everything freezes and nothing happens. Prior to the freeze everything in Zone 1 is covered in a red glow and surrounded by an impenetrable force field, nothing can enter or exit the zone, not even light, so the zone appears to the other zones as black. Once an hour has passed, the zone unfreezes. Events in Zone 1 continue as they had done before the freeze and the inhabitants of the other two zones can see that no change has occurred despite the passing of an hour. However, for the inhabitants of the frozen zone, the arrival of the red glow and the force field are not followed by all change freezing, but by a series of abrupt disconnected 'changes'.

Similar freezes occur also in the other two zones at predetermined times with identical results, and every thirty years there is a period where the whole planet freezes for an hour. The inhabitants quickly come to calculate exactly when the freezes will occur and modify their perceptions of time accordingly. Shoemaker seems to be suggesting through his hypothetically freezing world that time is the more fundamental aspect in the time/change relationship, and that far from time ceasing to exist without change, change can cease to occur whilst time continues.

If a tree falls in a forest and no one is around to hear it, does it make a sound?

The question 'if a tree falls in the forest and no one is around to hear it, does it make a sound?' is often attributed to the Anglo-Irish philosopher and clergyman George Berkeley (1685–1753). Although not a total misappropriation, the modern wording of the question differs somewhat from Berkeley's original proposition.

George Berkeley is considered to be the founder of a branch of philosophy termed subjective *idealism*. Idealism, in philosophical terms, states that reality as we know it is fundamentally a construction of the mind and our faculties of mental perception.

Berkeley's general thesis is that 'to be is to be perceived':

> *The objects of sense exist only when they*
> *are perceived; the trees therefore are in*
> *the garden no longer than while there is*
> *somebody by to perceive them.*
>
> GEORGE BERKELEY, *A TREATISE CONCERNING*
> *THE PRINCIPLES OF HUMAN KNOWLEDGE* (1710)

According to Berkeley's formulation, perception creates our reality and what we regard as physical things, including bodies, are nothing more than relatively stable and regulated patterns of perception. These patterns and mental constructions are assigned words and ordered into categories such as 'tree', 'cat' or 'rock'. However, our perception of these categories is immediate and 'in the moment'. Although Berkeley doesn't analyse his question (and never mentions sounds at all), his answer to the question would be that if a tree falls and no one hears it, then not only does it not make a sound, but furthermore 'the tree', insofar as it is perceived by the human mind, ceases to exist at all.

Opponents of Berkeley's point of view may claim that this suggests the absurd conclusion that trees go out of existence when no one is in the forest perceiving them. Science tells us that trees and forests exist, however, and furthermore, science tells us that trees have existed longer than humans have existed. So why does the existence of trees rely entirely on the perceptive faculties of the people perceiving them?

Berkeley avoids this conundrum by claiming that because God is omnipotent he is eternally present in the forest (as in all other locations) and, by always perceiving the trees, ensures their continuing existence. In other words, by lovingly holding all collections of perceptions within the divine mind, God ensures their continued existence: hence the perceived regularity of the 'natural world'.

> ❝ Reality leaves a lot to the imagination. ❞
> JOHN LENNON, QUOTED IN *SUNDAY HERALD SUN* (2003)

Therefore Berkeley's philosophy can be rendered into two levels of existence. On one hand, the level of an individual human body and mind, the level in which our perceptions create reality. What we perceive via our senses determines what we experience, and therefore what, for us, exists. On the other hand, there is the 'ultimate level' of existence in which God's simultaneous perception of everything ensures the continuous functioning of a shared 'natural world'.

Is too much better than not enough?

One of the most misunderstood schools of thought of Ancient Greece is *Epicureanism*. Often erroneously interpreted as unabashed self-indulgence in the pursuit of sensual pleasures, Epicureanism was in practice a form of measured asceticism.

Epicurus (341–270 BCE), the founder of the school of thought, was a disciple of an earlier teacher and philosopher Democritus (460–370 BCE), one of the principle thinkers of the *atomist* school. *Atomism* was an attempt to comprehend the changing nature of the universe and centred on the idea that everything is composed of atoms floating inexorably inside an infinite void. These tiny particles of matter move around constantly attaching and detaching themselves to each other to form different entities and bodies within the void. Democritus is often referred to as 'the laughing philosopher', with several commentators (Democritus' teachings survive only in second-hand accounts by later writers) noting his fondness for maintaining a positive outlook on life as a means of promoting spiritual wellbeing. Epicurus further expanded on Democritus' assertion that goodness is something internal to the human soul by developing a form of what has become known as 'ethical hedonism'.

Epicurus' ethical hedonism takes as its starting point Aristotle's assertion that 'happiness is the highest good' (see *What is happiness?*) and is valued for its own sake, not in relation to material things. However, Epicurus rejects Aristotle's equating happiness with pleasure and pleasure with the cultivation and practice of virtue. Epicurus took the view that the pursuit of pleasure was natural, innate and the driving motivation behind every thought and human action. An example of this natural predisposition for pleasure can be observed in the behaviour of very young children. Tickling babies or playing 'peek-a-boo' provokes laughter and smiles, and when these actions are suddenly withdrawn, the infant will often cry in response to the loss of the pleasure they were enjoying. Epicurus believed this inclination to seek out pleasure and avoid pain and loss is also naturally prevalent in adults but made more complex by factors such as social relations, systems of belief and notions of responsibility. These complicating factors, however, do not detract from Epicurus' basic contention that all activity is done for the sake of gaining personal pleasure, even actions that may appear to be self-sacrificing or provoked by duty. This is because the human capacity for introspection allows us instinctively to know that pleasure is good and pain is bad.

By linking pleasure with satisfying one's desires, Epicurus makes a distinction between two forms of pleasure: *moving pleasures* and *static pleasures*. 'Moving' pleasures relate to the action or process of fulfilling desires, for example, eating a delicious meal to satisfy hunger. Moving pleasures involve stimulating the senses to produce physical and emotional responses, and our sense of pleasure exists very much 'in the moment'. Epicurus argues that *after* the process, action or state has occurred and desires have been satisfied, we feel sated, as we are no longer in immediate need or want of anything. This state of satiety is a 'static' pleasure, and these hold an intrinsically higher value than moving pleasures.

The implication for Epicurus' distinction between the two states of pleasure is that there is no intermediate area between pleasure and pain. When needs and desires are unfulfilled this provokes pain, but once these needs and desires have been satisfied a state of static pleasure is realized.

❢ Enough is as good as a feast. ❢

JOSHUA SYLVESTER, *WORKS* (1611)

Epicurus also makes a clear distinction between physical and mental pleasures and pains. Physical pleasures and pains concern only the present (as exemplified by the yearning for, or realization of, moving pleasures). Mental pleasures and pains encompass both the present and the past, such as treasured memories of past happiness, or regret over past misfortunes and mistakes.

The main obstacle to achieving happiness, as outlined by Epicurus, is apprehension about the future. Taken in the context of his own time, Epicurus highlights the prevailing superstitions regarding fear of the gods and fear of death and the afterlife as the principle source of future anxiety. In order to reach a state of tranquillity (Epicurus uses the term *ataraxia*) it is necessary to displace fears about the future and face it with the confidence that one's desires will be satisfied.

Unsurprisingly, given Epicurus' concentration on the satisfaction of desires as the distinguishing factor between pleasure and pain, Epicurean ethics is devoted in the main to analysing different kinds of desires. If pleasure derives from getting what you desire and pain derives from not getting what you desire, then there are only two possible courses of action available: either strive to fulfil the desire, or endeavour to eradicate the desire. For the most part, Epicurus advocates the eradication of certain desires as the best strategy for achieving *ataraxia*.

Natural and necessary desires

Epicurean ethics outline three categories of desire, the first being natural and necessary desires such as the need for food and water, warmth and shelter. These desires provide the basic conditions of existence, so cannot be eliminated or subdued. Epicurus points out that these essential desires have a natural limitation, in that the human body can only absorb a certain amount of food, water, warmth, comfort and so on.

Natural but non-necessary desires

Natural but non-necessary desires are those that are on one level still basically essential to survival, but are not indispensable. Rich and expensive food and fine, extravagant wine (think caviar and champagne) belong to this category. These desires can be subjugated, for dependence upon them will bring unhappiness, and more easily attainable alternatives exist.

Vain and empty desires

Vain and empty desires include those such as the desire for power and influence, wealth and fame, and so forth. These desires are not natural prerequisites for existence and so have no natural limitation. The desire for power and influence is difficult to fulfil and is not a static pleasure. When one achieves a certain level of power and wealth, one instinctively yearns for more. These desires, for Epicurus, are born of false beliefs developed by human societies that bear no actual relation to what we really need to make us happy.

Of the three categories of desire, Epicurus advocates treating the second with moderation and restraint and eliminating the third category altogether. The pursuit of happiness and tranquillity should therefore be a process of limiting our desires to those which are essential and easily satisfied and discarding those which are not. In answer to the question 'is too much better than not enough?', Epicurus would doubtless reply that both states lead to pain and unhappiness and that knowing when one's desires are satisfied is 'enough' in itself in order to maintain spiritual tranquillity. People should estimate things of value to their long-term self-interests and abstain from things that provide pleasure in the short term for this will, in due course, lead to greater pleasures in the future.

Is there a difference between living and being alive?

On the surface, the question of the difference between 'living' and 'being alive' appears to be a simple matter of definition and interpretation. Biological definitions of living organisms set out criteria which need to be satisfied in order for something to be categorized as alive. These cover aspects such as reproduction, respiration, growth, excretion, response and so on. Philosophers, by and large, have been less concerned with the physical nature of simply being alive and have engaged themselves with metaphysical enquiries into the 'meaning' of existence. This search for the meaning of life has typically included ideas of happiness, morality and virtue, on both an individual and collective level. Whereas simply 'being alive' can be defined in biological terms as fulfilling certain essential necessities for survival, actually 'living' concerns matters of the reasons and values that can be ascribed to life. One philosopher who took an individualized approach to the question of what constitutes really 'living' was the nineteenth-century German Friedrich Wilhelm Nietzsche (1844–1900).

One of the central concepts in Nietzsche's philosophy was his analysis of the self. The predominant and traditional view in Western philosophy and religion is that human beings' existence is twofold in nature. We have our physical, corporeal bodies and our metaphysical minds. Nietzsche rejected this dual view of human existence and proposed the view that essentially mind and body are one. What people refer to as the mind or even the soul is merely an aspect of the physical existence of humans. In his episodic philosophical novel, Nietzsche wrote:

> *Body am I, and soul' – thus speaks the child. … But the awakened and knowing say: body am I entirely, and nothing else; and soul is only a word for something about the body.*
>
> FRIEDRICH NIETZSCHE, *THUS SPOKE ZARATHUSTRA* (1883)

The primary driving force behind these entities (bodies) and thus the value attributed to human life was to be found in what Nietzsche termed the 'will to power'. This is basically an extension of Arthur Schopenhauer's (whom Nietzsche greatly admired) somewhat pessimistic view that human life is dictated by a primordial 'will to live', the need to procreate and the battle to survive. These essentially physical aspects of existing or 'being alive' were, for Schopenhauer, the root cause of the suffering and unhappiness in the world. Nietzsche shifted the emphasis away from the 'will to live' as being a negative motivation and instead presented his will to *power* as a positive motivation and resource of human strength.

Nietzsche posited the theory that in the classical age moral values, both personal and societal, derive from the conflict of the good in the world (which were alive in the epic values of strength and power) and the bad (personified by the poor, the weak and the sick). This opposition is termed by Nietzsche as a form of master *morality*. For Nietzsche, organized religions such as Christianity developed a counter ideology to 'master morality' that he terms *slave morality*. This counter ideology is pivoted on a moral distinction between the good (ideas such as charity, piety, humbleness and restraint) and the evil (concepts such as cruelty, selfishness, dominance and wealth). Slave morality also promoted the idea of the soul as separate from the body and something to be judged by a higher consciousness (namely God). By subjugating the natural will to power as the driving force that provides meaning to life, slave morality was able to impose values that promoted subservience. As a result, heroic values of strength, ambition, individuality and creativity came to be seen as inherently evil and bad.

> 6 Do not fear death so much, but
> rather the inadequate life. 9
>
> BERTOLT BRECHT (1898–1956)

The question then for Nietzsche is that the difference between being 'alive' and 'living' is intrinsically linked to an individual's goals. Nietzsche takes particular issue with following any path in life according to meaning which is granted *a posteriori* (that is, derived from reasoned deduction) as this leads towards a negation of creative thought. The question of the meaning of life is reframed as not trying to come to conclusions or absolutes as to why human life exists at all, but why individuals exist:

> *... why you, individual, exist, this ask yourself, and if no one can tell you, then try to justify the meaning of existence* a posteriori *by setting for yourself some purpose, some goal, some 'therefore', a high and noble 'therefore'. Perish in pursuit of your goal – I know no higher life-purpose than to perish in the pursuit of something great and impossible ...*
>
> FRIEDRICH NIETZSCHE, *UNTIMELY MEDITATIONS* (1873–76)

The difference between living and being alive, for Nietzsche, was the duty of the individual to set themselves goals by creatively embracing the will to power. These individual goals should be 'high' and 'noble', and they should demand the best of the individual. Nietzsche weighs up the consequences of a self-defined meaning of life for a world inhabited by individuals. As there can be no pre-existing reason for existence which hasn't been tainted by moral codes imposed by false beliefs and determined entirely to satisfy their own ends, then the world in and of itself has no meaning. To be alive is to exist but to live or be living requires self-determination.

Nietzsche took a very iconoclastic approach to the

traditional philosophical quests for meaning and understanding, knowledge and method. His tendency to deliberately refute some of the sacred cows of philosophical thought such as Hegel's formulation of the dialectic and the validity of Socrates was a scatter-gun approach he deployed to questions concerning the meaning of culture, history, science, morality and art. Nietzsche's way was to reject the usual commonplaces, deny that there is a generally binding answer, and demand the primacy of individual interpretation, a method that has proved very attractive and influential. Although Nietzsche produced a dazzling array of contradictions and blind aphorisms, his texts were nonetheless always beautifully written and artfully conceited. Nietzsche's philosophy wilfully defies definition, for he believed it was up to us to draw our own conclusions, regardless of notions of right or wrong which aren't our own.

Is it better to love than to be loved?

The philosophy of love in its variant forms has been a topic that has engaged thinkers across the ages. Typically, there have been attempts to distinguish between different forms of love, most notably in theology and religion, which draw distinctions between 'earthly love' between individuals and 'other-worldly love' between God(s) and his (their) subjects.

The Ancient Greeks divided the notion of love into three separate forms which they named *éros*, *agápe*, and *philía*.

❀

Eros

The first of these terms has been subjected to different interpretations. The original meaning equated *éros* with strong sensual and sexual desire, and yearning for intimacy. Plato refined this interpretation in the *Symposium* (see *Is beauty in the eye of the beholder?*). Socrates' discussion in the *Symposium* (dated *c.* 385–370 BCE) evaluates the superficial nature of instantaneous erotic desire, although concedes this as a starting point. It is through contemplation that a person will come to understand physical desire to be a shallow response to physical beauty. Over time, a person's love will shift from the physical realm towards a love and understanding of the soul of the object of initial desire. This process is what we mean when we speak of 'platonic' love being 'a non-physical love', in that it is an appreciation of the beauty of the soul, and this requires a journey of transcendence.

Agápe

If *éros* can be categorized in the realm of 'worldly love', then the second form of love, *agápe,* traditionally resides in the realm of 'other-wordly' love. The theological interpretation as outlined in the book of Corinthians in the Bible equates *agápe* with 'the love of God for man and man for God'. In the concept of God's love for his subjects, *agápe* is taken to be spontaneous and unconditional: love is not bestowed upon us a reward for our intrinsic values of righteousness but simply because God's nature is to love. In contrast to *éros, agápe* is not dependent upon responding to any perceived value placed upon the object of love, but is instead supposed to promote values in its object. This idea of the enriching value of God's love is prevalent in the writings of the philosopher and theologian St Thomas Aquinas (1225–1274). Aquinas was a devout follower of the writings of Aristotle and attempted to synthesize ideas from Aristotle's writings on ethics with Christian theology. In his work *Summa Theologica* (1267), Aquinas defines God's love (and by extension all forms of love, given that God is omnipresent) as 'a movement of the will towards the good'. *Agápe*, in this interpretation, states that it is better to love than to be loved, as the movement of your love (God's love) will make the object of your love a better person. The unconditional emphasis is a key facet of *agápe*, as beyond the purely theological interpretation this form of love also encompasses the unequivocal love of parents for their children, and notions of brotherly love.

Philía

The third form of love, *philía*, explores the virtues of friendship, loyalty and solidarity. The term is used by Aristotle in his *Nicomachean Ethics* (350 BCE) to describe the love we can have or should devote towards our families and our communities through virtues such as equality and kindness. Aristotle also uses *philía* in an abstract and emotive sense to describe the love one can feel through experience. For example, the feelings stirred by music and art or the beauty of nature. For Aristotle the practice of *philía* was essential in order to live a virtuous and fulfilling life and so this view also contends that it is better to love than to be loved.

> ❦ It is better to be hated for what you are than to be loved for what you are not. ❧
>
> ANDRÉ GIDE, *AUTUMN LEAVES* (1949)

Not all philosophers have approached discussing the philosophical implications of love in a positive way. The Epicurean philosopher Lucretius (99–55 BCE) in his epic philosophical poem 'On the Nature of Things' (50 BCE) describes love, albeit in the sense of *éros* as destructive to personal virtue: 'love-sick ... life's best years squandered in sloth and debauchery.'

Nietzsche on love

Scholars of Friedrich Nietzsche are divided on the great German philosopher's views of the concept of love. Nietzsche remained a bachelor his entire life and is not known to have had any lasting or significant relationships with women. This has led some commentators to suggest Nietzsche may have been homosexual. Other commentators point to the fact that Nietzsche proposed to the same woman, Lou Salomé, on three occasions, but was rejected each time. There is even the suggestion that his distinctive bushy moustache was cultivated to hide facial features of which Nietzsche was extremely self-conscious. The following extract suggests a very cynical attitude to love, equating the concept of love as the desire for possession and therefore being transient in nature:

> *The lust of property, and love; what different associations each of these ideas evoke! – and yet it might be the same impulse twice named: on the one occasion disparaged from the standpoint of those already possessing (in whom the impulse has attained something of repose, who are now apprehensive for the safety of their 'possession'); on the other occasion viewed from the standpoint of the unsatisfied and thirsty, and therefore glorified as 'good'. Our love of our neighbour, – is it not a striving after new property?*

And similarly our love of knowledge, of truth; and in general all the striving after novelties? We gradually become satiated with the old and securely possessed, and again stretch out our hands; even the finest landscape in which we live for three months is no longer certain of our love, and any kind of more distant coast excites our covetousness: the possession for the most part becomes smaller through possessing. Our pleasure in ourselves seeks to maintain itself by always transforming something new into ourselves, – that is just possessing. To become satiated with a possession, that is to become satiated with ourselves. (One can also suffer from excess – even the desire to cast away, to share out, may assume the honourable name of 'love.')

FRIEDRICH NIETZSCHE, *THE GAY SCIENCE* (1882)

Do we have a soul?

The idea of the human soul, in religion and philosophy, has traditionally centred on the immaterial (non-physical) features of a human being that define individuality and sense of self. In religion, the notion of a soul is linked to a sense of the afterlife and, although it is incorporeal, many religions contend that the soul lives on after death. For the Ancient Greeks, the human soul related to our psyches, the 'voice inside our head', and as such formed the basis for our decisions and actions. In *The Republic* (*c.* 380 BCE) Plato outlines what he sees as the three essential components of the human soul.

The logical

The logical (*logistikon*) part of the soul is the area concerned with clarity of thought and the search for truth and understanding. The logical determines our capacity to reason and distinguish between what is real and what is false, what is right and what is wrong. This aspect of the soul regulates and governs the other two elements of our souls and is devoted to goodness. In religion, this element of the soul is akin to the Christian concept of righteousness, the pathway which leads the good and the just souls to heaven after death.

※

The spirited

Plato's second element of the soul is the spirited (*thymoeides*). This part contains the emotions that drive us and is where we feel anger or injustice. There is a clear difference between Plato's use of the term spirited and our usual notion of 'the spiritual'. Plato uses the term spirited to mean powerful feelings which must not be allowed to dominate us and need to be channelled towards goodness. In the just or righteous soul, the spirited works in harmony with the logical to curb the excesses of the third element, the appetitive.

The appetitive

The appetitive (*epithymetikon*) element of the soul aligns with our desires and search for pleasure. These desires can include the thirst for power and influence or base physical desires for the pleasures of the flesh. An unjust soul is one that allows the appetitive to dominate and ignores the guiding influence of the logical. In a religious sense, a soul consumed by the appetitive is incapable of resisting temptation and indulges in the sins.

For Plato, humans are the sum of their souls. They have physical bodies, but their nature is determined by their souls, which contain all the facets of their psychological capacities that determine their actions.

> ❧ Living is being born slowly.
> It would be a little too easy if we could
> borrow ready-made souls. ❧

ANTOINE DE SAINT-EXUPÉRY, *FLIGHT TO ARRAS* (1942)

In the seventeenth century, René Descartes developed a philosophical argument known as *dualism* that was closely related to notions of the soul. For Descartes, the mind and the body were separate entities, not as one. The mind, according to dualism, is composed of non-physical matter, as distinct from the physical matter of the brain. The mind is therefore placed into the realm of consciousness or self-awareness. The brain, being an organ of the body, belongs to the body, whereas the mind is separate. It is in the realm of the mind that our soul (self) resides:

> *Thus this self – that is, the soul by which*
> *I am what I am – is completely distinct from*
> *the body and is even easier to know than it,*
> *and even if the body did not exist the soul*
> *would still be everything that it is.*
>
> RENÉ DESCARTES, *DISCOURSE ON METHOD* (1637)

The nineteenth-century American philosopher William James (1842–1910), in his *Essays in Radical Empiricism* (1912) took issue with the concept of Cartesian dualism that views bodies and minds as fundamentally distinct. Drawing on his studies in human psychology, James posited what he termed a 'philosophy of pure experience'. For James, humans do not experience mind in separation from body, all they experience are the relations between thoughts, and bodily responses to those thoughts (such as sensations and emotions). This reduces the idea of consciousness as something separate and substantial to a mere illusion created by our minds. Our souls, therefore, are just ideas and not an entity in and of themselves. Our thoughts and our bodily perception of things are essentially the same entity, which James labelled 'pure experience'.

James's concept of 'pure experience' has echoes in modern developments in the discipline of neuroscience. Modern psychology dismisses the idea of the soul as separate from the body and places it firmly as an object of human belief, a psychology concept shaping our understanding of the natural world around us. In his theological writings, William James made a distinction between 'the healthy-minded' Christian and those with 'sick souls'. The healthy-minded view the world with optimism, believe in the greatness of God and the after life. Those with 'sick souls' question their beliefs, doubt the veracity of God yet continue to practise their religion despite hardship and despair. The mind versus body problem in philosophy is at the root of the question, do we have a soul? Perhaps the answer is we do have a soul, in a religious and spiritual sense, if we choose to believe that we have one.

William James and the bear

William James was a noted psychologist and in 1884 he published a controversial paper titled 'What is an Emotion?'. James put forward the idea that our experiences of emotion and sensation follow a set pattern of events preceded by some sort of physiological (bodily) stimulus. James put forward a hypothetical example of someone walking in the woods alone when they are suddenly confronted by a ferocious and angry-looking bear. The person turns and runs away in fear and blind panic. James posits the question: does the person run away from the bear because they are frightened or does the person feel frightened because they are running away? The traditional view would be that the bear provided the stimulus for the fear but James argued that this common-sense interpretation is wrong. For James, physiological changes in the body precede emotional perception or mental articulation of our emotional responses. The person runs away, which increases their heartbeat and neurological signals to the brain, which in turn cause the person to panic and provoke the psychological feeling of being afraid. In short, James believed different events and situations trigger different physiological changes, which in turn lead to different perceptions of our emotions.

Should duty come before pleasure?

The ethical philosophy of Immanuel Kant is based around the concept of duty. Since Plato and Aristotle, ethics in philosophy has revolved around the interpretation and definition of words such as virtue. Plato classified four *cardinal virtues*: wisdom, justice, fortitude and temperance. Aristotle later developed a list of more than twenty other characteristics that determine the Greek concept of *Eudaimonia* (well-being or living a 'just' life). Aristotle also placed certain virtues as the 'mean' point between two vices in a quasi-mathematical sense. For example, the Greek quality of courage is balanced between cowardice on one side and belligerence on the other. The virtue of temperance is taken to mean controlling one's base desires and so, as one of the cardinal virtues, it took precedence over the pursuit of pleasure for pleasure's sake.

Kant introduced his ethical theories by evaluating what we mean when we talk about virtues and asking whether it was possible to form a hierarchy of the moral worth of human characteristics, as with Plato and

Aristotle. Kant's conclusion was that the only virtue that can never be doubted or subject to question is the virtue of good will:

> *Nothing in the world – indeed nothing even beyond the world – can possibly be conceived which could be called good without qualification except the good will.*
>
> IMMANUEL KANT, *GROUNDWORK OF THE METAPHYSICS OF MORALS* (1785)

Kant argues that none of the other traditional virtues (such as benevolence, loyalty, valour, intelligence) hold the same status as good will, for the lesser virtues can be corrupted i.e used to achieve immoral ends. For example, it is possible to exhibit a veneer of kindness as a means of personal gain or to maintain loyalty to someone who is evil and cruel. In Kant's view good will is unique, in that it is goodness for goodness' sake and therefore maintains its moral value. This is true regardless of outcomes or the intentions or inclinations behind actions undertaken with good will as their premise. In this sense, good will remains a guiding moral principle even when it fails to achieve its moral intentions.

Kant's ethical philosophy also encompasses a notion of duty and the duty of individuals to do what is right according to reason (see *How can we tell the difference between right and wrong?*). However, Kant's notion of good will is not as formularized as his ideas about perfect and imperfect duties. A will which acts from duty surpasses obstacles or satisfies problems in order to maintain the moral law determined by reason. Take, for example, a person putting themselves in danger in order to save the life of another. A dutiful will is, then, a singular example of the exercise of good will that is only apparent or valid in difficult conditions. Kant extrapolates that only acts derived from this definition of duty have true moral worth. Although, in a sense, duty within these narrow confines could be said to limit human choice, and on occasion compels individuals to act contrary to their natural inclinations; nonetheless, they ultimately act in accordance with their own volition and the desire to uphold moral law and do what is right. When an individual is prompted to act from a sense of duty it is because the rational motivation to do what is right overpowers any other personal inclination. Kantian ethics thus attempts to move away from the idea that morality consists of a set of externally imposed values and virtues and presents an argument whereby all truly autonomous individuals should, if they think about any given situation, be able to recognize that through the exercise of good will and duty they are acting in accordance with moral law.

❝ When I'm not thank'd at all, I'm
thank'd enough: I've done my duty,
and I've done no more. ❞

HENRY FIELDING, *TOM THUMB THE GREAT* (1730)

The German philosopher Georg Wilhelm Friedrich Hegel (1770–1831) proposed two fundamental objections to Kant's notions of good will and duty. Hegel's principal argument centred on the fact that Kant's ethics provides specific consideration of what it is that people should actually do when they exercise good will and argued that this is because Kant's moral law is constructed on the principle of non-contradiction (where something cannot be true and untrue at the same time). This means that there is only ever one true course of action. So, to return to the question of whether it is better to act out of duty than pleasure, due to a lack of detail or consideration of circumstance Kant's moral law cannot constitute an absolute principle of morality. In essence, the formulation of an absolute of moral law (duty before pleasure, for example) doesn't give any meaningful answers, due to the abstraction of any discernible variables in context. By illustration, Hegel took issue with Kant's example of lending or borrowing money.

Kant believed that a person needing to borrow money from a friend shouldn't pledge to pay it back if they know they haven't the means to honour their promises. Hegel questioned whether Kant's principle of moral law was able to determine whether a social structure based upon property could ever categorically claim to be essentially morally good. It is interesting to note that much modern political philosophy focuses on the moral worth of money. In a challenge to relate strictures of logic and reason to Kant's ethics, Hegel also used the example of giving charity to help the poor.

Hegel contended that if everyone gave money to the poor in accordance with reason and, as Kant suggested, the principle of good will and duty, then there would no longer be any poverty. This seems to be a peculiar distortion of logic. Although rhetorically this might seem to undermine the absolute moral truth of duty and good will and render them redundant, it actually precedes Hegel's second criticism. Not everyone will help the poor, they simply won't do it for any of a variety of reasons. Hegel believed that this was fatal flaw in Kant's system because it forced humans into an internal clash between reason and desire. Hegel believed it was unnatural for the human mind to reject and suppress desire in favour of reasoned concepts such as good will and duty. The real question of this ethical dilemma lies elsewhere. If duty corresponds to what is the right thing to do in a given situation, then it appears to be the correct course of action. But if pleasure can alleviate suffering or pain, and duty has been corrupted by external pressures, surely it holds that pleasure should come before duty?

❛ How many people would like to be good, if only they might be good without taking trouble about it! They do not like goodness well enough to hunger and thirst after it, or to sell all that they have that they may buy it; they will not batter at the gate of the kingdom of heaven; but they look with pleasure on this or that aerial castle of righteousness, and think it would be rather nice to live in it. ❜

GEORGE MACDONALD, *PAUL FABER, SURGEON* (1878)

Are there universal truths?

The idea of universal truths suggests some things are constant and invariable, and represent unalterable facts. It could be said to be an absolute truth, for example, that there are no cats that are dogs, or dogs that are cats; that a square cannot be round and something circular cannot be square. This is to say that there are some things that are in reality static and cannot change, so can be considered to be universally true.

> ❝ The facts of nature are what they are,
> but we can only view them through the
> spectacles of our mind. ❞
>
> STEPHEN JAY GOULD,
> *BULLY FOR BRONTOSAURUS* (1991)

The quest to identify absolute or universal truths is linked to discovering the validity of statements and propositions. Aristotle defined truth with the following formula:

> *To say of what is that it is not, or of what is*
> *not that it is, is false, while to say of what is*
> *that it is, and of what is not that it is not, is*
> *true.*
>
> ARISTOTLE, *METAPHYSICS* (*c.* 350 BCE)

Or, in other words, we can say that a cat is a cat and a cat is not a dog and be stating a truth, but to say a cat is not a cat or a cat is a dog would be stating a falsehood.

This area of logic is known as correspondence theory, which holds that the truth or validity of statements of fact is determined by how accurately they correspond with reality. In the late nineteenth century, Bertrand Russell developed and analysed the different strands of the correspondence theory of truth. Russell's view was that our sense of reality was composed of our understanding of logically independent facts. Knowledge of things is dependent upon the information we have acquired through our direct experience of them. In relation to determining the truth or falsity of propositions (taking as a starting point that all statements, true or false, start from propositions), in order to determine their meaning we need to recognize the terms relating directly to our levels of acquaintance with the objects themselves.

Russell suggested two ways in which humans develop familiarity with objects and things. The first is 'knowledge by acquaintance': that is, information derived from our senses, perception of colours and forms, memories and so on. The second is 'knowledge by description': information from secondary sources which can only be inferred by or subjected to reason, but not directly experienced, including by experience of the object itself.

In his paper 'On Denoting' (1905), Russell outlined a quasi-mathematical approach to determine the truth, falsity or meaningfulness of statements and propositions. Russell noted that one of the problems with determining truth relates to the notion of definite descriptions. A description categorized as definite usually contains the definite article 'the', or a proper noun (a name with an initial capital letter). Russell used as his example the statement 'the present King of France is bald' and argued that the validity of the proposition was determined by the relationship between three distinct parts of the statement. In order to demonstrate the need for harmony between the three elements Russell broke the statement down:

There is an X.
X = the present King of France.
Nothing other than X can equal the present King of France. X is bald.

BERTRAND RUSSELL, 'ON DENOTING' (1905)

The definite description is comprised of two elements, that X is 'the' King of France and that he is 'the present' king (not 'a' previous king). The other element is that X is bald. Russell contended that all three elements need to be related in order to create an appearance of truth. If one element is out of harmony, then the statement is false. Interestingly though, the statement still has meaning even if one element is out of kilter with the other two. If the proposition is reworded as 'the King of France is bald' the relations between the elements in the description, although seemingly 'definite' are actually arbitrary as our descriptive knowledge of the subject tells us that there have been many kings of France. In this regard, any evaluation of absolute truth becomes more a matter of how language is used in propositions and the elements of a proposition are defined (which is a matter of description).

Russell's views on the philosophy of truth and its relation to language were preceded by Friedrich Nietzsche in a work called *On Truth and Lies in an Extra-Moral Sense*, which was written in 1873 but unpublished in Nietzsche's lifetime. Nietzsche was primarily concerned with the relationship between truth and language in the context of how we form concepts. For Nietzsche, words become concepts as a means of articulating a uniformity of experience, to facilitate communication. The problem for Nietzsche is that the relationship between words and the concepts they denote does not provide definite descriptions but metaphorical ones, which are in themselves arbitrary. A dog is a dog only in as far as we have attributed the metaphorical word dog to the concept of the animal we are familiar with. Thus, for Nietzsche words and concepts are merely metaphors, which do not correspond to their 'true' reality. With a typically self-consciously literary flourish, Nietzsche, having declared that absolute truths cannot exist, defines the concept of truth in the following terms:

A mobile army of metaphors, metonyms, and anthropomorphisms – in short, a sum of human relations, which have been enhanced, transposed, and embellished poetically and rhetorically, and which after long use seem firm, canonical, and obligatory to a people: truths are illusions about which one has forgotten that this is what they are; metaphors which are worn out and without sensuous power; coins which have lost their pictures and now matter only as metal, no longer as coins.

FRIEDRICH NIETZSCHE, *ON TRUTH AND LIES IN AN EXTRA-MORAL SENSE (1873)*

The idea of truth as a metaphor to describe a form of social currency (beautifully rendered by Nietzsche as 'coins which have lost their pictures') was to prove very seductive and influential to French postmodernist philosophers such as Michel Foucault and Jacques Derrida in the 1960s and 70s.

❝ Truth in philosophy means that concept and external reality correspond. ❞

GEORG WILHELM FRIEDRICH HEGEL (1770–1831)

What are 'the means of production'?

Karl Marx (1818–1883) was, in many respects, one of the most influential modern philosophers in the field of political thought. Marx's major work *Das Kapital* (1867) is considered to be one of the first systematic dissections of the economic structures that underpin industrial societies. Central to Marx's analysis is the concept of the mode of production, which relates to the explicit organization of economic production in modern societies. One aspect of the mode of production is the means of production, which includes resources such as industrial complexes, raw materials, sources of power and energy resources, agricultural facilities and manual labour. It also includes labour and the organization of the labour force. Marx also described what he termed relations of production: in short, the relationship between the group in society who have ownership of the means of production – the bourgeoisie – and subjugated groups who do not have access to the means of production, including the labour force of said production – the proletariat. Marx held that the history of human society springs from the interaction between the mode of production and the relations of production.

Capitalism can be defined as a mode of production predicated on the means of production being under the private ownership of a small, wealthy elite. These elite use the means of production to produce commodities to sell and exchange in distinct but interconnected markets. The competing forces within these markets make it necessary to try to produce commodities for the lowest possible cost, which in turn entails the wholesale exploitation of the labour force (the workers or proletariat). It is in the interests of capitalists to pay workers the bare minimum in order to survive and be productive. This causes friction between the proletariat and the bourgeoisie and gives rise to a historical struggle between the classes within the relations of production. Marx believed that this class struggle would eventually manifest itself in the dismantling of the capitalist system and the birth of a new system of collective ownership of the means of production known as communism.

❝ What is Communism? It is that when you have eaten enough food for your hunger and still food is left – it belongs to another man. ❞

A. R. MURUGADOSS, *KATHTHI* (2014)

Marx's early work drew heavily on Hegel, and in particular Hegel's notion of the dialectic. Hegel's model is essentially a description of how human thoughts and ideas evolve through a process of synthesis between two conflicting perspectives. Marx was a materialist and believed that human beings define themselves through the things that they create through their work (or labour). In a capitalist system the worker becomes alienated and estranged as they hold no stake in the means of production and this separates them from their most basic mode of existence and sense of identity. The fruits of labour for Marx were integral not only to satisfy basic instincts for survival but to project personal identity and a sense of self-worth. Capitalism denies the worker this capacity for self-creation through their labour and strips people of their identity, alienating them not only from themselves but also from each other. Through their labour, human beings transform materials into objects or things that have value according to their usefulness as commodities. Labour allows humans to satisfy their most basic needs and to project themselves on to the world. Private ownership of the means of production separates humans from this process of self-creation and labour becomes instead merely a means to an end and a struggle for survival, for the products of labour are expropriated by the bourgeoisie and sold for personal profit in order to maintain the economic interests of an elite minority. This process of alienation separates humans from the essential process of transforming objective matter into objects or things of use-value, which Marx placed as a fundamental facet of human life and experience. Denied the opportunity of a collective stake in the fruits of one's labour, the alienated proletariat view their capitalist masters as 'other'. This antagonistic class struggle will naturally be resolved by overthrowing the capitalist system and replacing it with collective ownership of the means of production.

The influence of the writings of Hegel is most noticeable in Marx's concept of historical materialism. For Hegel, human consciousness can be defined as an evolutionary process or journey tracing the development of thoughts from simple ideas to complex systems. The human capacity to articulate thoughts began with very simple and basic attempts to understand the nature of objects in the world and has progressed, through a dialectical process, to higher and more abstract forms of consciousness. History, according to Hegel, is also subject to this dialectical process, as each civilization develops and builds upon the conflicts and contradictions of previous ages. As ideas are the principal means by which human beings understand the world, the history of the world is essentially the history of these ideas, how they have evolved and developed over time and how their contradictions are challenged and resolved on a conceptual level. The Marxist view of history adopts the idea of the dialectic, but differs from Hegel's view in that it is based not on idealism but on materialism. For Marx, historical epochs can be understood by looking at the structures and methods of social organization that a particular society or civilization adopts, and how this relates to human beings' most basic material needs and requirements. History, for Marx, is therefore grounded in historical materialism and can be viewed as the evolution of different economic systems and modes of production, created to cater for our basic material needs but inevitably leading to conflicts and the creation of new social systems that also evolve over time.

The Bombing of Karl Marx's Tomb

The tomb of Karl Marx in Highgate Cemetery in London was erected on the site of his grave in 1955. The imposing plinth and bust by sculptor Laurence Bradshaw was paid for by voluntary contributions from The Communist Party of Great Britain, and attracts hundreds of visitors every year. The tomb has, however, been vandalized on several occasions and was the subject of a bizarre bomb attack on 18 September 1970. Recently released police files describe how the vandals used a home-made bomb comprised of fireworks and weed killer and attempted to saw through the head of the bust to place the bomb inside the statue. This plan failed, as they were unable to cut through Karl Marx's nose and opted instead for detonating the bomb at the foot of the plinth. Although crudely constructed, the bomb was powerful enough to shatter some paving stones and cause six hundred pounds' worth of damage to the marble plinth. The culprits were never caught and no political activists or groups have claimed responsibility for the bombing.

Are there questions that science cannot answer?

To ask whether there are questions that science can't answer would appear to be committing something of a conceptual oxymoron. The whole purpose of science, in the classical sense, is bound up in the quest to know the hitherto unknowable. There are, of course, many things that science is unable to fully explain, instead relying on postulating hypotheses and theories. The idea that science should be able to lend explanations for everything from natural phenomena to human behaviour is known in philosophical terms as positivism.

Positivism is a philosophy of science based on the idea that the only legitimate knowledge is scientific knowledge. According to this school of thought, the social sciences (such as sociology, psychology and anthropology), in keeping with the traditional sciences, can be subjected to the rigours of collecting empirical data and applying mathematical logic to such data to determine truths. By obtaining, analysing and validating the data garnered by empirical observation, science is able to formulate general laws. In short, if it can't be counted it can't be true. The positivist perspective also states that societies function by general laws in the same way that the physical world has general laws and principles such as the phases of the moon or the forces of gravity. Positivism rejects the validity of purely introspective or abstract thinking, so in this respect is opposed to theology and metaphysics. Although there are clear traces of positivist ideas in the work of earlier philosophers, most notably in the work of Francis Bacon, David Hume and George Berkeley, the term was first developed in the modern era by the work of the nineteenth-century French philosopher and father of the social sciences, Auguste Comte (1798–1857).

Between 1830 and 1842, Comte published a series of texts collectively known as *The Course in Positive Philosophy* (1842). Comte's early works describe epistemological perspectives in the physical sciences, which he then develops into approaches to analyse the mechanics behind human societies in general. Indeed, it was Comte who founded the term sociology for the study of societies. Comte's starting point was to attempt to rank the different categories of science according to what he termed their degree of positivity. Positivity as a criteria for assessment is essentially the extent to which particular observable phenomena can be exactly determined. This exactness is measured by the degree to which mathematical demonstration can be seen to provide clear and coherent proof. Comte concluded that there were five chief areas of scientific enquiry that, although of equal value to human knowledge, nonetheless could be classified according to a scale of diminishing positivity. Comte's scale, in decreasing order was: astronomy, physics, chemistry, biology and sociology.

It was to the last category on his positivity scale, sociology, that Comte turned his attention. He outlined what he saw as three phases of human social evolution since primitive times.

The theological phase

The theological phase lasted until the Enlightenment and is characterized and ordered by humanity's supplication to God and religion. Society is organized and suppressed by religious doctrines which are accepted for fear of exclusion or persecution in return for denying any rational attempt to address the basic questions of our existence.

The metaphysical phase

The second of Comte's phases of human social evolution, the metaphysical, began with the Enlightenment and ended after the French Revolution. The logical rationalism prevalent in this period gave rise, for the first time, to ideas about the primacy of human rights and the search for universal rights for all humanity to understand and abide by. This quest to understand the meaning of individual experience and the search for collective consciousness beyond the restrictive confines of religious doctrine inevitably led to conflict and war.

❋

The positive phase

The final stage is the age of science. Human society has evolved to understand its inner workings, the primacy of individual rights and the capacity to exercise free will and to self govern. The progress between Comte's three phases follows the 'universal law' of human social development – each phase must be completed before advancing to the next phase. The notion of an onward march of progress was key to Comte's theory, as progress requires evaluation of the past in order to build the future, and it is through science (and technology) that Comte's largely utopian vision will be realized.

One of the problems with Comte's three stages of the universal law of human social evolution is the question of when progress stops. Or, put another way, when does social ideology cease to progress (see *Has history ended?*)? For the positive stage to have been realized, science would, in a sense, have all the answers to all the questions.

Secondly, how would society know it was in the positive phase, since scientific research and development is an ongoing process? Furthermore, the insistence on measuring positivity according to that which can be most exactly determined through mathematical data derived from observation is questionably narrow and reductive. The German physicist Werner Heisenberg, a fierce opponent of positivism (see the quote overleaf) formulated what is known as the *uncertainty principle*. It is Heisenberg's assertion that the exact position and momentum of a particle in space cannot be simultaneously known. Or put another way, the subject of observation is directly influenced by the observer, thereby conforming to the principle of uncertainty in any assessment of exactness (or positivity). In this sense, at least for now, it seems that humanity is still very much in the metaphysical phase, as there are so many questions that science cannot answer.

❦ The positivists have a simple solution:
the world must be divided into that which
we can say clearly and the rest, which we had
better pass over in silence. But can anyone
conceive of a more pointless philosophy, seeing
that what we can say clearly amounts to next
to nothing? If we omitted all that is unclear
we would probably be left with completely
uninteresting and trivial tautologies. ❧

WERNER HEISENBERG, *PHYSICS AND BEYOND –
ENCOUNTERS AND CONVERSATIONS* (1971)

Do words have meanings?

Traditionally, philosophical attempts to ascertain whether words have meanings have centred on the idea that the definition of words (and hence their meaning) comes about from the interplay between the sign (written symbols or spoken sounds) and the object to which they refer. Thus the word 'dog' means a quadruped mammal of the genus *Canis familiaris*. In philosophical terms this is known as the *correspondence theory* of meaning. It stresses the notion that true ideas and statements, in order to have meaning, must correspond to their objects as they are and that related meanings must be in harmony with these ideas and statements. Therefore, the truth or the falsity of a representation (symbol or word) is dependent exclusively upon its relationship to things and whether it accurately describes them. The problem with correspondence theory is that it relies upon the assumption that there is an observable objective reality that can be accurately described by reference to symbols, sounds and thoughts. Modern philosophers have disputed the validity of the correspondence theory of meaning by pointing to how different languages function, and comparing their different processes and structures. Many languages, particularly languages from South-East Asia, have words which are identical in sound and symbol so that their meaning is deduced entirely from the context produced by their relative proximity to other words. Although this doesn't entirely dispute the basic notion that the true meaning of words is, in the words of St Thomas Aquinas, 'the equation of things and thoughts', it nonetheless suggests that the production of meaning in words is a complex process.

Ludwig Wittgenstein, particularly in his later writings, moved away from the idea of meaning being derived from reference and representation. The traditional view in analytic philosophy, prior to Wittgenstein, was to take a proposition or statement and ascertain its truth-value according to external aspects. These defining factors were either as objects in space (such as our dog) or mental representations in thoughts. Wittgenstein came to the conclusion that the idea of external referents endowing words with meanings was flawed, and that it was a case of looking in the wrong place. It was Wittgenstein's contention that the meaning of words was not to be found by correspondence to their referents (either physical or mental) but simply for what the words were being used:

> *... if we had to name anything which is the life of the sign, we should have to say that it was its use ...*
>
> LUDWIG WITTGENSTEIN,
> *PHILOSOPHICAL INVESTIGATIONS* (1953)

Wittgenstein's 'meaning is usage' is put to the test in his posthumous work *Philosophical Investigations* (1953), which was assembled from his copious notebooks and manuscripts. Wittgenstein structures the book around a series of thought experiments which he then unpicks with a series of conflicting propositions. For example, he sets up the hypothetical scenario of handing somebody a shopping list on which is written 'five red apples'. The shopper walks to a grocery store and hands the list to the shopkeeper who then goes to a cupboard marked 'apples'. He then pulls out a colour chart and looks up the word 'red', before counting out five correspondingly red apples. The traditional contention would be to ask (as Wittgenstein does): 'how does the shopkeeper know what the word five means?' Wittgenstein argues that how the shopkeeper understands the meaning of the word 'five' is not important in his scenario: the only important issue is that the shopkeeper understood how the word 'five' was being used.Wittgenstein further elaborates on his meaning as usage theory by drawing an analogy of words as representing a huge toolbox. When we look into a toolbox we recognize the objects as being of functional use – we may have no idea what some tools are used for, but we can recognize them nonetheless as tools. Likewise, other tools we may know have more than one use, and so the function and therefore the meaning of the tool changes in different contexts.

> For a *large* class of cases of the employment of the word 'meaning' – though not for all – can be explained in this way: the meaning of a word is its use in the language.

LUDWIG WITTGENSTEIN,
PHILOSOPHICAL INVESTIGATIONS (1953)

Wittgenstein's examples and contradictions eventually led him to the conclusion that the functions of language were analogous to playing a game. There are many different types of games, with many different rules and there are even games with no formal rules at all, but the important thing for Wittgenstein was being able to recognize the meaning usage that is inherent in the functions of language. We can recognize that chess and blind man's bluff are games and differentiate between them, but this is not dependent on having a clear set definition of the meaning of the word game: it is merely how the word is applied to different social contexts that dictates how it is being used, and therefore its meaning.

�֍

Wittgenstein's method for dog training

Ludwig Wittgenstein was famous during his two tenures at Cambridge University for wildly eccentric and erratic behaviour. During a meeting of The Cambridge Moral Sciences Club, an elite discussion circle of Oxbridge academics, Wittgenstein is alleged to have threatened the Austrian philosopher Karl Popper with a red-hot poker during an argument on the validity of moral rules. Popper claimed philosophical problems were real and related to how people live, whereas Wittgenstein claimed they were merely linguistic 'games'.

Wittgenstein's friend and biographer Norman Malcolm also tells of having a heated debate with Wittgenstein on the legitimacy of ostensive definition as a means of teaching language to infants. Ostensive definition is essentially a process of defining meaning through pointing out examples. Malcolm returned to his house one afternoon to find Wittgenstein in his garden with Malcolm's pet dachshund. Wittgenstein was bending over the dog with a stick in his hand repeating the sentence 'this is a stick, that is a tree' and pointing to an apple tree in the garden. According to Malcolm, Wittgenstein spent over an hour repeating the same sentence to the bewildered dog, who eventually got bored and wandered off. When Malcolm looked out of his kitchen window some time later he saw Wittgenstein lying on his back on the lawn with the stick between his teeth.

❝ What is rational is actual and what is actual is rational. ❞

GEORG WILHELM FRIEDRICH HEGEL (1770-1831).

Is there such a thing as destiny and fate?

In Greek mythology and literature – particularly the work of the great poet Homer – fate and destiny are regarded as fixed and pre-determined at birth. Fate was unavoidable and to accept and live through one's fate showed courage, whereas to attempt to avoid one's fate was sinful and likely to anger the gods. This concept of accepting one's fate with honour can be seen as a precursor to later ideas of Stoicism (see *Is the glass half full or half empty?*).

One pre-Socratic philosopher who rejected the traditional Greek view of fate was Heraclitus (*c.* 540–480 BCE).

Heraclitus was born in the Greek city of Ephesus, now in modern-day Turkey, and is considered to be the last of the great Ionian (that is, one of the four major tribes of Ancient Greeks) philosophers. There is scant information about his life other than anecdotal stories from the Greek historian Diogenes Laërtius in his *Lives and Opinions of Eminent Philosophers* (from the first half of the third century CE). Diogenes portrays Heraclitus as a misanthropic and melancholic figure, determinedly critical of his predecessors and peers. Heraclitus' philosophy survives in the form of around one hundred epigrammatically structured sentences that have the quality of riddles or proverbs. This often wilfully obscure form has led to conflicting interpretations of some of Heraclitus' pronouncements. However, despite his unconventional approach, there are clear concepts that Heraclitus returns to again and again, such as the unity of opposites and the philosophy of universal flux. At the centre of Heraclitus' thought lies the radical assertion of universal flux. This thesis posits that everything in the universe is constantly flowing and moving like an endless river. Heraclitus was particularly fond of this river analogy and is credited by later philosophers such as Plato with the famous aphorism:

Everything changes and nothing remains still and you cannot step twice into the same river.

HERACLITUS OF EPHESUS, *EPIGRAMS OF HERACLITUS*

Drawing upon his observations of the perpetual processes and elements of the natural world, Heraclitus described the world as 'an ever-living fire kindling in measures and going out in measures'. Fire was the key element for 'The death of fire is the birth of air, and the death of air is the birth of water.' In this regard, the universal flux that constitutes the world (and by extension, the universe as a whole) is a journey of everlasting transformations between the elements and so therefore 'all things are one' through this constant flow and interconnectedness.

It could be argued that claiming 'all things are one' in the universal flow negates the idea of difference. Heraclitus argues that difference and change depend upon the 'unity of opposites'. Day exists because of night, up exists because of down, black exists because of white, fire exists because of water and so on. The universal flow is maintained through the cosmological equilibrium established through the balance of opposites.

Heraclitus challenges people to accept that we live in a world 'that no god or human has made' or predetermined, and so this affects (in his own time at least) ordinary values and beliefs. He counsels that people should take a more detached view of life, that his audience should try to think away their purely personal concerns and view the world from his more detached perspective. By the use of metaphorical aphorisms and riddles, Heraclitus aimed to question the relativity of value judgments and beliefs, such as ideas of destiny and fate. The suggestion is that unless people reflect on their experiences and cultivate a mind based on wisdom, strength and self-determination, they are doomed to live a zombie-like existence which is not in harmony with the formula of universal flux that governs the nature of the universe.

❦ Character is destiny. ❦

HERACLITUS OF EPHESUS
EPIGRAMS OF HERACLITUS

The 'ever-living fire' therefore constitutes and symbolizes both the processes of nature in general but also the nature of the human soul. Heraclitus believed that the human soul, symbolically, was comprised of the elements of fire and water. As the source of life and thought, a 'fiery' soul gave people the necessary character for people to examine themselves and their actions, and through the process of reflection they could become at one with the formula of nature.

Heraclitus' notion of the fiery soul as part of the natural flow had important implications on the traditional Greek concept of fate. One of Heraclitus' most famous aphorisms states that 'Character is destiny' which seems to be at odds with the idea of a pre-determined fate or a power beyond our grasp. Heraclitus seems to suggest that the cultivation of a fiery soul is synonymous with the development of personal character and the ability to think deeply about our lives and the decisions that we make, therefore it is our character, not some incorporeal force, that determines destiny and fate.

> *'Character is destiny,' says Novalis, in one of his questionable aphorisms.*
>
> GEORGE ELIOT, *THE MILL ON THE FLOSS* (1860)

George Eliot and the German Poet

Eliot's use of the line has caused much debate amongst her scholars, not least because it is a misquotation. The Novalis to whom Eliot attributes the aphorism was the pen name of Georg Philipp Friedrich von Hardenberg, an obscure poet of the German Romantic movement in the late eighteenth century.

George Eliot (real name Mary Anne Evans) was a voracious reader as a child and had access to the library of Arbury Hall, the estate on which she grew up. Many of Eliot's novels incorporate ideas and motifs influenced by her love of Greek literature and philosophy, so it would seem likely that she was aware of the writings of Heraclitus. Some critics have suggested that Eliot's 'mistake' is a joke about Novalis' poetry and a deliberate trick aimed at her readers.

Has history ended?

The term 'the end of history' relates to a theoretical proposition in political philosophy that suggests humankind has reached the apotheosis of its social and economic development. In order to grapple with this audacious philosophy, it is important to separate the idea of history having ended with the idea of time ending, or apocalyptic prophesies of the end of the world that are prevalent in many religious doctrines or quasi-religious cults.

In 1989, the political theorist and commentator Francis Fukuyama published a controversial essay titled 'The End of History?' in the international affairs journal *The National Interest*. Central to Fukayama's thesis (expanded upon in his 1992 book *The End of History and the Last Man*) is the view that history itself is not a timeline of connected or unconnected events but an evolutionary process. The late 1980s saw the collapse of communist regimes in Eastern Europe, culminating in the fall of the Berlin Wall in November 1989. This heralded the end of the Cold War and the decades of nuclear standoff between East and West. For Fukuyama, the communist experiment, which Karl

Marx had predicted would naturally and necessarily supersede capitalism, had failed, leaving Western liberal democracy as the dominant social and political ideology that forms the basis for the maintenance of civil societies. Fukayama claims that modern history has, since the French Revolution (*c.* 1789–1799), been concerned with the development of conflicting ideologies of how society should be organized, culminating in the formation of Western capitalist democracies. It is not that history has stopped and there will be no more events, but that there will be no further developments in political ideology.

Fukuyama's theory sparked a furious debate amongst leading academics. For many left-leaning thinkers such as the French philosopher Jacques Derrida (1930–2004), Fukuyama's essay was nothing more than the triumphalism of a neoconservative keen to disparage Marxism and claim ideological superiority for free-market capitalism. To counter Fukuyama, Derrida points to the obvious inequalities prevalent in the world and the fact that this can be seen as a concomitant by-product of capitalism:

> *For it must be cried out, at a time when some have the audacity to neo-evangelise in the name of the ideal of a liberal democracy that has finally realised itself as the ideal of human history: never have violence, inequality, exclusion, famine, and thus economic oppression affected as many human beings in the history of the earth and of humanity.*
>
> JACQUES DERRIDA, *SPECTERS OF MARX* (1993)

Fukayama used the fall of the Eastern bloc and the rapid switch from command economies and one-party states to free-market democratic states as empirical evidence that liberal democratic systems had won the ideological war with Marxism that had dominated the post-war era. The fact that racism, poverty and inequality still exist in these liberal 'utopias' was unfortunate, but there remained no organized revolutionary movement to challenge the dominant ideology.

❝ The wind of revolutions is not tractable. ❞

VICTOR HUGO, *LES MISÉRABLES* (1862)

Is this cessation of socio-political ideologies actually true? The economic and military rise to power of one-party states such as China and North Korea and, to a certain extent, Russia under Vladimir Putin would seem to suggest that communism is far from dead as a social and political system. The Fifth Republic Movement of the former president of Venezuela, Hugo Chavez, demonstrated that popular support could still be utilized in the name of traditional socialism. Interestingly, Chavez directly attacked Fukuyama's end of history theory in an address to the United Nations General Assembly in 2006. Fukuyama responded by arguing that Chavez's socialist super-state was only possible by being bankrolled by the discovery of oil reserves in Venezuela at the time of Chavez's rise to political prominence, and was thus subsumed in capitalist ideology after all.

Fukuyama's end of history thesis has also been challenged in the wake of the attacks on America on 11 September 2001. The rise of Islamic fundamentalism with its clear antagonism towards Western liberal democracies is a clear example of vociferous and organized dissent. The financial crisis of 2008 also gave rise to the global Occupy movement that protested at financial centres in London and New York. Anti-austerity demonstrations across parts of Europe, although fragmented, nonetheless show that perhaps Fukuyama was a little hasty in claiming that history has ended and that there will be no further developments in the evolution of human social ideology.

End of History Versus Start the Future

The end of history debate had a part to play in a competition to create the world's strongest beer in terms of alcohol content. In 2010, the Scottish micro-brewery BrewDog produced a limited edition of twelve bottles of beer with an alcohol content of 55% ABV. The BrewDog company was founded by Martin Dickie and James Watt, who met whilst studying philosophy at Aberdeen University and named their world-record-breaking beer 'The End of History' in tribute to Fukuyama's controversial essay. The beer also attracted controversy and criticism from animal rights campaigners, as the bottles were set inside the carcasses of taxidermied squirrels and sold on the Internet for £750 each.

BrewDog only held the record for a couple of weeks before 'The End of History' was superseded by an even stronger beer, created by Dutch micro-brewery 't Koelschip (The Coolship). The Dutch company's 60% ABV beer was created using a revolutionary cryogenic fermentation method and, in a mischievous reference to their competitors, was named 'Start the Future'.

Is there life after death?

It seems slightly frivolous, when approaching the question of life after death, to simply recede into an agnostic position. Arch-pessimist Arthur Schopenhauer took a very nihilistic view of the subject of death, defined by his famous assertion that 'After your death, you will be what you were before your birth.' At least, that would appear on the surface to be Schopenhauer's view: we are born out of nothingness and when we die we return into a void of non-existence. Despite his notoriously gloomy outlook on life (see *Schopenhauer's Breakfast*), there is an underlying empathy in Schopenhauer's writing, a feeling that somewhere, somehow, there must be an escape from the unrelenting suffering of much of what constitutes human life. The following quote seems to suggest that the seemingly futile nature of loss should maybe be readdressed:

> *The deep pain that is felt at the death of every friendly soul arises from the feeling that there is in every individual something which is inexpressible, peculiar to him alone, and is, therefore, absolutely and irretrievably lost.*
>
> ARTHUR SCHOPENHAUER,
> *PARERGA AND PARALIPOMENA*, VOL. 2 (1851)

Schopenhauer was fundamentally a materialist in that he believed that the world was comprised of objects and that they must be constructed from material (the idea that when we conceive substance, we can only think in terms of matter). Schopenhauer believed that materialism could be related to idealism; that is, systems of thought in which the objects of knowledge are considered to be dependent on the activity of mind, or that the functions of the brain in individuals are material processes. This is a tricky tightrope to walk as it is a position between opposing ideas of materialism – that there is only matter, atoms, particles and things which are subject to the laws of pre-determination – or dualism – where the functions of the mind/soul are separate from the physical reality of the world.

Materialists argue that if we are nothing more than our physical bodies and death destroys our bodies, it follows that we cease to exist and there is nothing left of us as persons. Dualism seems to lend itself more readily to ideas of life after death. If we have non-physical (or immaterial) minds or souls and this constitutes us as persons, then even the total eradication of our physical bodies may not entail our complete extinction. One of the key theories in support of dualism contends that it is conceivable that the human mind can exist without a body, for our reliance on our bodies is conditional, or essential only according to our understanding of the present laws of nature. An omnipotent and omnipresent god created those laws and so is capable, as with resurrection myths, of violating the laws of the physical world.

One of the main objections to dualist theories of life after death centres on the problem of identity. When describing the identities of people we are not describing the identity of their souls. This is because, if we take it that souls cannot be perceived, as they don't exist in physical reality, how can we recognize them? Furthermore, what we take to be the identity of a person over a period of time cannot correspond to the identity of the person's soul over time. We can recognize and identify a person's body. However, once the person has died and the particles that make up the body start to break down and decompose, this body no longer resembles (for identification purposes) the incorporeal soul that is taken to have survived.

This presents a logical problem for materialists when considering the question of life after death, principally because there is an issue surrounding the preservation of personal identity. In dualist theology, personal identity is maintained through the resolution of the soul between death and resurrection or rebirth. Materialists argue that there can be no bridge between the body that has died and the body that is reborn. How can we be sure, therefore, that the body that has been resurrected is personally identifiable with the body that is deceased? Recreation theory suggests that God, or some higher power, rebuilds the person with identical characteristics to the person that has died. The epistemological problem at the heart of theories of recreation is that if we take it that God can rebuild bodies identical to their original form, what is to stop God making multiple bodies or copies of the same bodily form? How is the uniqueness of personal identity preserved in either physical or spiritual form? It seems hard not to view the resurrected 'person' as merely a replica, given that we exist at a given point in time, cease to exist and then are recreated. It begs the question why the process of death should be necessary in the first place?

> ❝ Life does not cease to be funny when people die any more than it ceases to be serious when people laugh. ❞
>
> GEORGE BERNARD SHAW (1865–1950)

The contemporary American philosopher Peter van Inwagen examined the fallacies inherent in recreation myths in his paper 'The Possibility of Resurrection' (1992). Van Inwagen outlines a hypothetical example based upon relics of saints in Catholic monasteries. In his scenario, a certain monastery claims to own a manuscript written by St Augustine. The monastery's history shows that Arian tribes ransacked the monastery in 457 CE and burned all its contents, including St Augustine's script. How, then, did the manuscript survive the fire? The monks reply that God recreated it in 458. Even if we are to take at face value God's miraculous intervention, the manuscript that God recreates cannot be the same as the one that was burned, because it wouldn't have existed in the world when St Augustine was alive. Nonetheless, the monks continue to insist that their manuscript is the same one written by St Augustine. The question therefore is the extent to which a recreation can retain its uniqueness, or is the act of recreation, in a sense, akin to cloning or producing replicas of originals? Van Inwagen, a devout Catholic, comes to the conclusion that maybe it is not possible to fully comprehend notions of life after death or recreation, simply because we do not yet possess the necessary conceptual resources. The belief in life after death, rebirth or resurrection is a central tenet to many religions and faiths. It can provide comfort and meaning to the existence of our earthly bodies and minds. Perhaps belief in life after death should therefore be taken as a matter of faith over reason.

Conclusion: in a nutshell

In the introduction to this book I ruminated on the nature of philosophy and asked whether it was actually possible to present it 'in a nutshell'. This book has attempted to present the philosophical thoughts and arguments of some of history's greatest thinkers as they attempted to answer those 'big questions' that occur to all of us from time to time. To some extent their answers (or perhaps better, responses, given that many philosophies do not answer questions at all in the traditional sense) have to be understood in the context of how they grappled with understanding and analysing their respective worlds.

In the seventeenth and eighteenth centuries, a clear shift moved the focus away from the more cerebral aspects of philosophical investigation towards scientific observation and experiment as a means of determining truths about the world and our experiences. The horrors of the twentieth century, the nuclear age and massive advances in technology seem to have relegated philosophy to the margins of human knowledge. Philosophy was then regarded as a purely academic pursuit: 'the history of ideas', rather than a practical study to be applied to everyday life. It could be argued that academics are to blame for this, as the rigid analytical frameworks of the age of reason were rejected in favour of obscure concepts and an ever-increasing use of bewildering terminology and specialized areas of study (such as hermeneutics and deconstruction) in the self-styled post-modern era.

We are living in an age where the distribution of information is becoming ever faster. The Internet and social media means that thoughts and ideas and opinions can be dispersed and exchanged with bewildering speed and regularity. In theory, this should be a good thing for the free exchange of ideas. If the object of philosophy is to ask questions and test arguments and propositions about human life and thought, the freedom of expression the information age allows should be a godsend. There are problems, of course, as the recent controversies surrounding surveillance and control of the Internet by government organizations and multinational companies has illustrated. Traditional ideas and issues of personal freedom could be resurrected in a whole new socio-political context.

Ecological and environmental issues will also present key questions and issues for the philosophers of the present and near future. Traditionally, Ancient Greek philosophy, particularly in the area of ethics, concerned itself with the question of how to live a virtuous and fulfilling life. The dangers of global warming, world poverty, famine and disease and sustainable energy resources have switched the emphasis away from the individual to the global question of how humans as a species can survive. This could therefore be the challenge for the philosophy of the future

Another key issue for future philosophers is the environment and the impact of global warming, in particular. 'How to live?', the key question addressed by all the great thinkers, shifts again in emphasis to ask, 'How can we live?' in this world hurtling towards a point of economic and ecological unsustainability. In this light, philosophy becomes a matter of not only understanding human knowledge and ethics, but something far more fundamental: ensuring the survival of civilization and safeguarding future generations. Perhaps those questions are philosophy in a nutshell?

Acknowledgements

I would like to thank the following people whose kindness, help and advice has been invaluable in compiling this book. Louise Dixon, for suggesting the project in the first place; my ever-patient and excellent editor Gabriella Nemeth; Charlie Mounter, and the design and production team at Michael O'Mara Books. R. Lucas and James West and the staff at the University of Sussex library for allowing me to use their facilities and fielding my queries. My wife, Joanna Taylor, and beautiful daughter Polly for letting me test out some philosophical conundrums and questions on them, and their continued love and support.

Selected Bibliography

Ayer, A. J., *The Central Questions of Philosophy* (Holt, London, 1974)

Blackburn, Simon, *Think: A Compelling Introduction to Philosophy*, (Oxford University Press, Oxford, 1999)

Blackburn, Simon (ed.), *Oxford Dictionary of Philosophy* (Oxford University Press, Oxford, 2008)

Cahn, Stephen M., *Exploring Philosophy: An Introductory Anthology* (Oxford University Press, Oxford, 2008)

Craig, Edward, *Philosophy: A Very Short Introduction* (Oxford University Press, Oxford, 2002)

Critchley, Simon, *The Book of Dead Philosophers* (Granta, London, 2009)

Gaarder, Jostein, *Sophie's World* (Weidenfeld & Nicolson, London, 1991)

Grayling, A. C, *The Meaning of Things* (Weidenfeld & Nicholson, London, 2001)

Kaufman, Walter, *Existentialism from Dostoyevsky to Sartre* (New American Library, New York, 1975)

Kohl, Herbert, *The Age of Complexity* (Mentor Books Ltd, New York, 1965)

Levine, Lesley, *I Think, Therefore I Am* (Michael O'Mara Books Ltd, London, 2010)

Mautner, Thomas (ed.), *Penguin Dictionary of Philosophy* (Penguin Books, London, 1997)

Monk, Ray and Raphael, Frederic, *The Great Philosophers* (Weidenfeld & Nicholson, London 2000)

Nagel, Thomas, *What Does It All Mean?* (Oxford University Press, Oxford, 2004)

Pirie, Madsen, *101 Great Philosophers: Makers of Modern Thought* (Bloomsbury, London, 2009)

Russell, Bertrand, *History of Western Philosophy* (Allen & Unwin Ltd, London, 1961)

Singer, Peter, *The Life You Can Save* (Random House, New York and London, 2010)

Suits, Bernard, *The Grasshopper: Games, Life and Utopia* (Broadview Press, London, 2005)

Urmson, J. O. and Rée, Jonathan, *The Concise Encyclopedia of Western Philosophy & Philosophers* (Routledge, New York and London, 1989)

Warburton, Nigel, *Philosophy: The Basics* (Routledge, London, 2012)

Index

The perfect companion to

Why We Think the Things We Think . . .

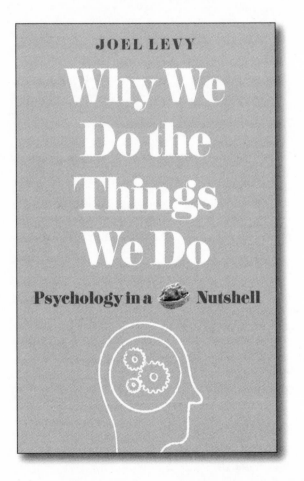

ISBN 978-1-78243-412-2
in hardback print format
£9.99

ISBN 978-1-78243-410-8
in ebook format